TEA & BEE'S MILK

Also by Karen and Ray Gilden

How to Plan Your Trip to Europe (Artha Press, 1995)

KAREN AND RAY GILDEN

TEA & BEE'S MILK
OUR YEAR IN A TURKISH VILLAGE

Artha Press

www.teaandbeesmilk.com

Artha Press
Monmouth, OR 97361

ISBN 978-1-886922-10-5 (electronic)
ISBN 978-1-886922-12-9 (paperback)

Photographs by Ray Gilden, © 1987, 1993, 1996, 1997.
Map of Turkey on page 217 courtesy of the University of Texas.
Cover design by Joanne McClennan.

Printed in the United States of America.

www.teaandbeesmilk.com

For Mom and Dad who gave their blessing
and for Jennifer who encouraged us,
Rick and Beverly who invited us,
and Sue and Jim who kept the cat.

Contents

TEA & BEE'S MILK

Preface

Sometime during December of 1995 we got a fax in the middle of the night. It told of an apartment for rent for one year, furnished, in the small village of Göcek on the Mediterranean coast of Turkey. The rent was cheap and the location was appealing. We had been to Turkey twice before and knew we liked it. Our daughter was grown and on her own, and our jobs were—well, just jobs. So, why not go?

This book is a memoir of our year in Turkey. It is drawn primarily from weekly emails to friends at home, and letters and other sources; the narrative framework was added later. We hoped to publish it on our return but our lives grew chaotic and busy and it didn't get done—until now.

Since leaving Turkey we've had other adventures: a road trip from Oregon to Yucatan, crisscrossing Mexico for six weeks in a little white Dodge Colt; a cross-country camping trip in a VW bus from Newport, Oregon to Boston, Massachusettes on US highway 20 and return; and many, many trips to France, where for six years we owned a little house in Languedoc. We have not been back to Turkey since we left in 1997, but it holds a special place in our hearts and we still hope one day to return.

The possibility for misunderstandings and errors are rampant when writing about a culture that is not one's own. The views and ideas expressed in this book—as well as its errors—are strictly our own. Some names have been changed to protect the anonymity of friends and acquaintances.

This book would not have been written without the encouragement of friends and the help of many. We would especially like to thank Ellye Bloom, who edited the original manuscript and without whose comments and suggestions it might not have seen print. We greatfully acknowledge the proofreading assistance of Gwynne Spencer, Mary Anne Zabawa and Tony Marciniec.

Turkey is often misunderstood by Americans, but this friendly and fascinating culture is well worth knowing. We hope this book will spark your curiosity and that some insight, some fragment of humor or history, encourages you to see for yourself what multi-faceted Turkey is all about.

Karen and Ray Gilden
Portland, Oregon

Should we have stayed at home and thought of here?
Where should we be today?
Is it right to be watching strangers in a play
In this strangest of theatres?

—Elizabeth Bishop, 1911–1979

SUMMER

Four bags and a bus

July 11, 1996

The heat is intense and the breeze coming off the sea offers no relief, it simply blows dust and debris into swirling eddies at our feet. The open-to-the-sky bus station is a crush of jostling, sweaty travelers; noisy, idling diesel engines; and competing hawkers calling destinations.

"Fethiye, Fethiye, Fethiye!" shouts the driver as we pull our four overloaded bags to the side of the midibus.

"Göcek?" we ask. "Göcek, yes," he confirms.

Gratefully, we turn our luggage over to the driver's assistant and climb aboard. The bus looks almost new and a sign indicating air conditioning immediately cheers me. Underway, though, it's clear the air conditioning is more imaginary than real and that the weak overhead vents and open bus doors will be the only source of relief. The seats in this little bus are narrow so I'm squished between Ray and the window with the computer bag and two hats at my feet. Why did I bring two hats?

It's so hot I can't stand anything touching me. I elbow Ray, whose five-foot, ten-inch frame suddenly seems oppressively large.

"Move over!" I plead, but he also has a bag and a hat at his feet, and nowhere to move.

"Will you just relax?" he says. I grit my teeth and try to shake some air into my sweat-soaked tee-shirt, and then I close my eyes against the bright, bright light and wonder what I'm doing on a bus in Turkey.

Pounding nails into clouds? Coming here sometimes seemed as senseless but opportunity, in the shape of a furnished apartment in a sunny coastal village, had presented itself and we couldn't resist. I was 54 and Ray was 57 and if we'd had a banker she would no doubt have been appalled, a financial adviser agitated, a retirement counselor aghast at our precipitousness. None of those specialists stood nearby, however, and financial security was ours to risk. We examined our stress-filled lives, found them increasingly constricted and stale, and thought the risk worth taking. Secure tedium might be prudent but freedom looked like a lot more fun.

Fixating on freedom we quit our jobs, sold our 100-year-old house and four-year-old car, shared out the family heirlooms, found a haven for the cat, and jammed the rest of our belongings into a 12x20 storage unit. It was tough to leave friends and family but my parents, in their mid-eighties, graciously gave their blessing and our daughter promised to visit in December.

Turkey itself was a known and appealing quantity in this freedom vs. security equation. Our love of travel had brought us here previously—for three months in 1987 and three weeks in 1993—and we were eager to renew acquaintance with the country and with old friends.

We waved goodbye to Oregon on a cool July morning and arrived in Turkey in the middle of a summer heat wave, exhausted from the strain of packing and leaving, and the days of travel, but happy to be where we were. We had no income, but no debts; no home, but no responsibilities. Now we had only our suitcases—two bags each—a camera and a laptop computer to worry about. We had, in the jargon of the day, simplified.

The laptop computer is resting on my feet now, heavy in its black canvas case stuffed with books, spare disks, and accumulated "important" documents. I shift its weight, move the hats again, and stare out the window. The little bus bumps over the narrow, two-lane highway, its low-powered diesel engine straining as we creep up the curving hills and humming efficiently as we race down the other side. During the slow, uphill climb, the hot air congeals and presses heavily on my bare limbs. On the downhill side it's obligingly carried away by the hot gusts that stream in through the open front door and out the open back. As we and the other passengers lurch and gasp between hot, jelling air and sweeping blasts of hot wind, we are accompanied by the dissonant wail of Turkish pop. This is not restful music. Maybe the heat has affected it too; the notes sound melted and they're oozing from the bus speakers.

Still climbing we chug past roadside stands selling pine nuts and "bee's milk," as the attendant moves sideways down the narrow aisle offering water to drink or lemon-scented cologne to splash on our hands, face, and neck. This is all the relief we're going to get, it appears, for the cooler temperatures we had hoped to find in the mountains don't materialize, and even the pine trees languish and droop.

At Muğla the bus makes a 20-minute stop, and we stretch our legs in the shade of a building and buy another bottle of cold water. Back aboard we turn south, and with the change in direction my mood improves. This is new territory, and the new vistas are, as always, revitalizing. The architecture too has changed. The flat-roofed, white-cube houses of the Bodrum peninsula and ancient Caria have been left behind and we've arrived in ancient Lycia, a land of white bungalows and red-tiled roofs. The landscape has changed too. It's greener, there are more trees, and the terrain is steeper and more rugged. From Muğla the road winds steeply down a mountainside, and through pine-covered slopes I glimpse the highway traversing a flat plain far below, and in the distance the Mediterranean Sea. Definitely new territory.

As we descend toward the plain the air grows damper, heavier, and hotter. Farms and villages now line the highway and our progress slows, interrupted by stops and starts as a steady stream of passengers boards and departs. With each stop the bus grows hotter and my patience shorter, though I love Turkey's slow, relaxed pace. It is, in fact, one reason we succumbed so quickly to the lure of spending a year here. Exhaustion opens the door to apprehension and my tired brain recycles its worries: our rent has been paid 12 months in advance and we're going to a place we've never been, to live in an apartment seen only in photos. Did we act too hastily? Are we being foolish? What if it turns out to be a miserable place? What if we hate it?

I look at Ray, intently watching traffic through the bus's front window. His face shows the strain of the last few weeks but he's engrossed in the sights surrounding us, obviously enjoying the flashes of life and color that flow past the windows. He's as eager a traveler as I am, certainly a more outgoing one, and I know he's looking forward to the year, and to the cheerful hospitality we've always found here.

Reassured, I watch as we roll past groves of orange and lemon trees, past farmhouses and fields and villages. Eventually the bus shifts into low gear and crawls up a last high range of hills, and as it starts down the other side we catch a glimpse of "our" village far below. Then, abruptly, we're there, climbing stiff-legged from the bus, warily taking in the bright heat, the humidity, and the unfamiliar surroundings. We collect our bags and watch as the bus—which I'm suddenly, unaccountably fond of—pulls back onto the highway. Then we turn to see Tom, our new landlord, strolling toward us.

He's tall and smiling and we're happy to see him, but the scene feels disorienting. The movie reel has slipped, or a page has been pulled from our animation sequence. For a split second everything is remarkably clear and glisteningly brilliant. Then the fog of exhaustion settles again and I hear Tom asking about our bags. Do we want a taxi? No, we can manage. With his help we gather our things for the last leg of the journey and trudge off together toward our new home.

We half-pull, half-carry the bags down a gently sloping street, turn left at a taxi stand, and plod over a flat, bumpy dirt track past a large, half-poured concrete slab, toward the white, three-story building that is our goal. The closer we get the more discouraged I feel, and by the time we reach the rough cement front steps and the unfinished hallway, with hanging rebar and gaping plaster holes, holding a smile on my face is an effort.

"This is not important," I tell myself. "It's just how things are."

Our introduction to Tom's wife, Emma, and to the apartment, passes in a blurred haze of exhaustion, trepidation, and relief at having finally arrived. Neighbor's names, oven instructions, and shopping advice all melt into the bottomless pit of what was my memory. Finally, after arranging to meet later for dinner, our hosts return to their home for the coming year, a 45-foot sailboat they are taking east toward the Pacific.

When the door closes behind them I immediately burst into tears. Recalling the extensive view from our Bodrum apartment ten years earlier—a vast, uninhibited expanse of mountains, castle, harbor, sea, and in the distance the Greek island of Kos—I feel deeply disappointed. No one had mentioned that in Göcek we would have a view of a construction site, with its attendant noise and dust. The apartment is modern, light, and comfortably furnished, just as the photographs showed. But it is still chock full of their personal belongings. How can we ever make it feel like our home, surrounded by so many of their things? Tables are covered with knickknacks and mementos; a collection of hats and stuffed animals rests on the hall étagère, and a wall of family photographs dominates the office. When I look about and see a year of endlessly dusting someone else's treasures my tears go to flood stage.

Ray, who's as tired as I am, is now faced with a near-hysterical wife. He gives me one of those everything-will-be-all-right hugs, and says, "Relax; this place will feel like home in no time—you know it will. Right?"

"Right," I mutter reluctantly into his chest, adding, for the umpteenth time, "Do you think we're doing the right thing?"

"Absolutely," he says, adding with down-to-earth finality, "Let's unpack. I need a shower."

The apartment

At home in Portland, struggling to complete the thousands of details our plans demanded, I had indulged in dreams of idyllic simplicity. I could hardly wait to leave our possessions behind, along with the stresses and strains of U.S. life in the 90s. Like Thoreau, I wanted to trim life to the bone and get down to the basics. I imagined the quiet peace of a country setting. I anticipated elegantly simple meals prepared with a minimum of fuss and few implements. I saw myself spending long evenings with a book in plain and restful surroundings. The photos Tom sent us of the Göcek apartment were lost in the mail for months, and by the time they arrived the image I had conjured was too powerful to be negated and at that point it didn't matter; we were committed. What awaited me though was not my longed-for Levantine Walden, but the west transferred. Yet I could hardly fault Tom and Emma for bringing their belongings from England, or for wanting their home to be comfortable.

If one were to judge only by the interior, the second floor apartment might have been anywhere. It had a roomy, well-equipped kitchen with more cookware than we could ever use; a moderate-sized living room with fireplace; two bathrooms, one with a shower, the other with a shower and a tub; a small master bedroom, and another used as a den/office. (A third bedroom was locked, being used for owner storage.) Two small balconies, one in front and one at the side, were furnished with a table and chairs for dining or relaxing, and a rack for drying wet clothes. We had all the important appliances: a hot-water heater, a dishwasher, a clothes washer, a microwave, and a telephone.

The furnishings in our new home were "English"; floral patterns and clutter being what I most associate with English rooms. The living room alone contained a small dining table and two chairs, a three-drawer chest of drawers, a television and VCR, a narrow, upright stereo cabinet, two matching sofas—called settees by their owners—covered with floral print, two huge leather swivel chairs and a matching ottoman, four brass table lamps sitting on four glass-topped end tables, a matching coffee table, a Turkish tray-top table, a plant stand, and a small, brass-trimmed wooden trunk. Every table secured a number of decorative whatnots; 16 on the coffee table, eight more on an end table. A pale green carpet overlaid by a couple of small Turkish rugs anchored all this, with copper pots and too many paintings completing the decor.

The two-year-old building was constructed in the usual Turkish style. Built of large but fragile-seeming hollow bricks (locally called breeze bricks), it was plastered and whitewashed and topped with a red tile roof. Throughout the building the doors and window frames were knotty-pine. In our unit the floors were also pine, except the hall, bath, and kitchen floors, which were red tile. And as I discovered almost immediately, tile is an unforgiving receiver of delicate china.

Our unit was one of six. By law, buildings in Göcek are not to extend above two stories, but the wily Turks get around this by turning the attic space under the eaves into another floor. Thus our building had four large apartments; two each on the first and second floors, separated by a central hall and staircase, and two smaller apartments under the eaves on the third floor. We were sandwiched between, on the second. Above us lived Mehmet (one of the property owners), his wife Aygul, and their three-year-old daughter Ipek. Below us was Huseyin, a single bachelor. Huseyin, we found, spoke passable English, but Mehmet and his family knew little.

Opposite us on the same floor was the apartment that Tom's sister and brother-in-law, Helen and Bob, used as a vacation home. It was vacant when we arrived but we were told to expect them in about six weeks. The small flat above them was rented by two English women—known as the two Judes—who visited only a few weeks each year. Below Bob and Helen on the ground floor lived a constantly changing group of young singles who, as near as we could determine, worked for one of the yacht chartering agencies in town.

Finding the apartment so densely furnished was a blow, but not an irreversible one. Eventually we packed most of the whatnots and some of the smaller pieces of furniture into the spare bath and when Helen and Bob arrived from England they happily accepted the loan of a sofa and end table. Then we rearranged the furniture, set a couple of family photographs on the mantle, and called it home.

As we became acquainted with our accommodations we discovered the oddities that make every dwelling unique. Comparing notes, we realized that each time we put our hands under the kitchen tap we were rewarded with a sharp, prickling feeling. Ray traced this to an electrical short in the dishwasher, so we unplugged that convenience and washed the dishes by hand, gaining one step toward simplicity.

The clothes washer was an Arçelik, a modern Turkish machine only a few months old and, as I wrote to a friend, it was unusual, with no fewer than 10 separate cycles:

A   cotton with pre wash

B   cotton—normal

X   gentle

M   small load

C   spin—normal

D   synthetics with pre wash

F   synthetics—normal

G   gentle—30° (centigrade)

J   wool;

H   spin—short

P   empty.

"The Arçelik" I wrote, "has several unique features, but the primary one is that it lacks a start button and you must know which incantation to recite before it works. I usually start with abracadabra and end with the F word.

"Here are the operating instructions (translated from Turkish):

Load machine

Put soap powder either in machine or drawer [we use Omo, not forgetting a soup spoon of Calgon to soften the water]

close door

select program

select temperature

select wash: normal, half, crease guard.

"These instructions must be followed *precisely*. It takes an orderly mind to remember to put soap in the drawer before you close the door, not after; and certainly one must never select a temperature (86°–200°F) before selecting a program. If you do, the Arçelik will simply sit and look at you. It has all the time in the world, you see; just like a Turk. I've had long discussions with this machine, sitting on the floor reopening and closing doors and resetting dials, and even when I'm sure I've done it correctly Arçelik may just sit there. I've reached the conclusion that some programs like to have the door slammed harder than others, or maybe they like the program dial set *after* the temperature. Like all good magicians, however, Arçelik never tells its secrets, and I am left to squat on the floor in front of it repeating incantations until it chooses to start.

"Once started (breathe a sigh of relief and spin counter-clockwise three times) a cycle can last from over one hour to nearly two. It may spin for ten seconds, stop for 30, spin for 15, stop for 20, or 60, and then, perhaps, run for five minutes before stopping and starting again. There is undoubtedly wisdom in this design for the clothes do get clean, but unlike American machines that run their course and then rest, this one operates like the Turks in this way too: it works, has a tea break; works, has a snack; works, has another tea break and maybe a visit; works, has lunch; works—until finally the job is finished.

"When the wash is complete we have only to remove the laundry and hang it to dry. This is simple if one remembers that Arçelik expects to remain in charge to the bitter end. To empty: 'Turn temperature dial to off position. De-select wash. Wait two minutes. Open door.' Be sure the machine is finished before you do this, because its habit of stopping midway to rest can be deceiving. We avoid arguments by adding an additional 30 minutes to the estimated wash time. Everything takes longer in Turkey."

A few words about a small village

Everything does take longer in Turkey, with one dramatic exception: seaside villages turn into coastal resorts almost overnight. A dozen or so years ago Göcek was the quiet home of a few hundred people; a scattering of houses and tiny shops bordering a beach of pebbles and sand. A couple of beach-side cafes catered to the occasional yacht or *gulet* that anchored in the bay. There were one or two *pansiyons*, a campground, and a collection of vacation cabins, but visitors were more rare than common, and they had little effect on the life of the village.

The residents lived as they always had. A few worked at loading and unloading the ships that carried chrome ore from a nearby mine, and a few more proffered the services that every village needs. Most people fished and farmed, raising fruit, vegetables, and goats. Then Göcek was discovered.

Word spread among Turkey's elite—among them then-president Turgut Özal—that the little village at the foot of Fethiye Bay was a special place. Inevitably, the well-publicized presence of prominent visitors brought more yachts into the bay and more people into the village. This encouraged the building of shops and restaurants that cater to tourists, and their presence in turn brought more. The completion a few years ago of nearby Dalaman airport made it quicker and easier for tourists to reach Göcek, and the cycle continues to expand.

Despite the changes, the village is still charming. Walking out to dinner on our first evening, with Tom and Emma beside us, we were struck by the beauty of the site. The bay spreading away from the curved promenade was blue and clear, and the surrounding mountains crowded the dusk-dark sea. Still dazed by the heat and the long trip, and by the finality of finding ourselves bound to this unknown place for an entire year, we attended only slightly to the recommendations and injunctions of our hosts. As we made our slow circuit through the little town I knew I should pay attention to their reports on various shops, and the names of the numerous people we met, but I couldn't. I was too tired, and too dizzied by the variety of restaurants and bars that lined the quay, the colored lights that blazed from every direction, and the fashionable tourists and traditional Turks who strolled in confusing profusion along the promenade.

Besides, grateful as I was for their help, I wanted to make my own discoveries and draw my own conclusions. Tom and Emma's Göcek I knew, would not be ours. They had a five-year history in the community and called it home; we were new and temporary residents. Göcek would be ours for only a single, brief year and I wanted my impressions unmuddied by the influence of others, no matter how well-intended. Besides, at the moment it was taking all my energy to remain upright.

July 22

The tourists here carry an air of anticipation and excitement with them, and their multinational backgrounds add a level of sophistication not usually found in places this size. Most of the visitors have chartered sailboats for a week or more, and we've come to enjoy strolling along the promenade, watching the new arrivals. They laugh with relief and sigh with exhaustion and suck on beers while they unpack and stuff their gear into the sailboat's lockers. Then they trundle off to the grocery store to purchase supplies. Their vacation giddiness billows and spreads through the town and makes it a happy place to be. Despite this cheerfulness we're looking forward to November, when they and temporary workers will be gone. Then we'll get a glimpse of Göcek as it used to be.

The village occupies land that was once under water, but for centuries the Mediterranean has been slowly receding and this spot—once, perhaps, a silent, shallow cove—is now a busy, flat, waterlogged little plain. To exit the town, therefore, one is forced to go up, and the mountains we travel over are rust red and steep, covered with pine trees, pink-blooming oleanders, bright red hibiscus, and other unidentifiable—at least by me—shrubbery.

These steep mountains also surround Fethiye Bay, which is the big attraction here. It's a large body of water well sheltered from the fierce summer winds. It's almost impossible not to want to spend all your time on a boat, for there are 12 seductive islands nearby, all with quiet coves for anchoring or swimming, and a few with ruins to explore. The result of this abundance of watery perfection is that yachts of every size and flag come here from all reaches of the Mediterranean.

It's a short walk from our apartment to Göcek's principal street and this is a good thing since we have no car. The street starts at the highway near the bus stop and runs gently downhill. We join it near the taxi stand, just before it crosses a narrow stream. Once across the road divides into two; one branch turns sharply left and heads northeast, back to the highway. The other becomes a neat, gray-brick road that runs between a few old houses and many small shops and restaurants. If you stroll this route you'll undoubtedly find yourself engaged in a conversation—it's as certain as the sunshine.

"Where are you from? Do you like tea? You want carpet? Come and sit down, please."

That little *bufe*, where the two men are playing backgammon, is a good place to buy beer and wine. Over on the left is our favorite grocery; Ilhan, the young man in charge, spends most of his waking hours there. On the right are shops selling pottery, jewelry, kilims and more. The larger shop is a favorite of local expats who often stop in for tea and gossip. And there are two pharmacies, just opposite one another, with all the sunscreen you could need.

The little gray-brick street parallels the waterfront for a few short blocks and ends in a gray-brick square. From here it's only a few steps to the mosque, the grammar school, the post office, and the sea. Turn right at the square and walk past the grocery, the spice stall, the news stand, the souvenir and clothing stores, and between the two big restaurants, and you're onto the wide, stone-paved promenade that edges the Mediterranean. If you happen to be here on a weekend you'll see Turkish families strolling arm in arm in the evening light, and a fleet of blindingly white charter yachts bouncing and rolling in water that splashes against the concrete retaining wall.

The yachts that line the wall and the piers, that float at anchor in the harbor, or appear as white wisps on the horizon, are Göcek's *raison d'être;* bringing shoppers and money into town. There are now in this village at least eight small grocery stores advertising "yacht service," and 10 to 15 restaurants. On a personal level that means lots of good food. There are several yacht charterers, six or eight *pansiyons*, a couple of hotels, many bars, two marinas, three piers, and lots and lots of tourists.

It hasn't taken long to feel at home here. The foreign residents are amiable and the Turks are justifiably praised for their hospitality. Though it's hard for Americans to accept—we're a suspicious lot and think anyone this nice must have an ulterior motive—they are genuinely friendly and helpful. You'll have to throw your skepticism and preconceptions aside, because there's a gentleness and warmth in the Turks that deserves your consideration. Of course they'd love to sell you something too.

The pide maker

Swimming in history

The community we found ourselves in was so different from the one we had left that I sometimes felt I'd landed on the moon. Yet it held the same familiar elements: families and houses, cars and streets, dogs and cats, mountains and seas. This familiarity often camouflaged deep differences in attitudes, making it harder to perceive the truth of our surroundings. Though we had visited Turkey twice before, had driven the length of its Aegean coast and traveled inland through mountains and across high plains, we had much to learn.

Our Turkish language skills were mediocre, incomplete scraps forged years before. We had tried to study before we left home, but study kept sliding to the bottom of our to-do lists. Fortunately Emma owned a number of language tapes and books, and we pulled them off the shelves and diligently began to listen and practice. Neither of us has an ear for languages and hours of study have never brought more than minimal mastery. Turkish proved to be no exception. Unlike English, it does not depend on word order to make sense. Instead, sentence meanings and parts of speech are reflected in changing syllables and suffixes that can be added and added, producing long melodious vowel chains that are lovely to listen to but impossible to follow. At least for me. Our *Berlitz Turkish Phrase Book* offers this example as one, "with which the Turks themselves like to startle foreigners." *Avrupalilastirilamiyanilardanmisiniz?* Meaning, "Are you one of those who can't be Europeanized?"

Luckily for us English is widely spoken along Turkey's coasts. Some of our Turkish friends were fluent in English, but most knew only the words and phrases necessary to speak with tourists. Still, that was often more than we knew of Turkish, and our attempts to speak in that language were usually met with replies in English. I found this frustrating at first but eventually it gave me an excuse for doing what I wanted to do, which was to not study. I mastered all the courtesy words, numbers, and phrases I could, then reverted to osmosis as a way of learning more. Ray persevered, however, and by the time we left he could communicate pretty well, as long as the subject was primarily mercantile.

Exhaustion, coupled with the unfamiliar and intense heat, made our first weeks quiet ones, but we gradually began to find our way into the community. One of the first steps was to locate a place to swim and cool off. Except for a dirty, grainy beach west of town the water nearby was either inaccessible or crowded with boats, but eventually someone told us about the beach across the bay.

July 30

We went swimming yesterday. Frankly, it's too hot and humid to do anything else; we barely move, we wilt on the couch or melt onto the tile floor uttering prayers to the ice goddess who never answers. Swimming is our only relief, and since we do this fairly often I will tell you about it.

First we stop to buy a borek from the stall near what we call the hardware store. A borek is made of dough that is rolled like a large, very thin flour tortilla, or crepe, and cooked on a round, flat pan. Then it's folded around a filling, usually goat cheese and herbs like parsley and dill. If you think of it as a Turkish burrito you won't go wrong.

Carrying our boreks we ride our bikes to the small ferry that departs Skopea Marina every odd-numbered hour. Yesterday we took the 11 a.m. ferry, tomorrow we plan to go at nine. Sharp on the hour—you can hear the young captain's watch-alarm beep if he's lounging nearby—the little ferry powers away from the dock, enveloping its passengers in diesel smoke as it turns sharply south to weave its way through anchored yachts to the other side of the bay and Club Marina.

Club Marina is a private marina in a sheltered harbor. Large boats often moor here, and it's more elegant and considerably more expensive than the town pier. One section offers separate docks for each yacht, parking for the owner's autos, and room for flower pots and tables and chairs and barbecues. Of course the big boats don't really need room for flower pots and tables and chairs, etc., because some of them are so big they have trees on board and no one ever seems to leave the bar anyway.

After we unload our bikes (often the young captain helps) we maneuver them along the stone path in front of the Marina restaurant ("Sunday *bufet*, TL1,000,000, 8:30–11 p.m."), up four steps, and onto the graveled single-track road. From here we pedal the half mile or so to the end of the point protecting the harbor. We lean the bikes against the red rock cliff, or maybe the flagpole, and walk another hundred yards or so across gravel and rocks and a low man-made wall, to a small rocky beach under a bluff. And this is where we swim.

All this traveling cuts into our swimming time. It's about a ten minute trip across the bay and another five minutes from the restaurant to the beach. This is important because due to the ferry schedule (it returns to Göcek on even hours) we have to decide whether we want to go for a one-hour swim or a three- or five-hour swim. Usually we opt for the shorter one but occasionally we bring food and stay longer, or go through the Club and up the road to another cove with a nicer beach. Of course we also have the option of riding both ways, or one way, but the road is pretty bad and the heat and humidity are pretty bad and so the ferry looks pretty good.

This is a good beach for boat watching (I should say yacht watching because in Turkey every boat that's not a *gulet* or a fishing boat or a dinghy is a yacht) and yesterday was an especially good day because it was Saturday and there was lots of traffic. Two boats we had been tracking for a week were gone, somewhat to our relief. These were identical motor yachts—big enough to have trees aboard—and like women caught wearing the same dress at a party, they kept to opposite sides of the bay and different moorages. The British boat out of Hamilton was called *Headlines* and naturally we speculated on which newspaper mogul owned it. The other carried one of the more tasteless names we've seen: *Honey Money*. Perhaps this is not surprising since it was registered in the Cayman Islands.

The high salt content in the Mediterranean makes swimming a relaxing affair. One floats with almost no effort and I have to remind myself to move and get some exercise. Yesterday I lay in the water with my feet up and my arms outstretched, looking across the bay toward the high peaks that stand over the town of Fethiye, 35 miles away. The water was choppy because of all the boat activity and I was just lying there, rocking on the little waves and admiring the view and I suddenly remembered where I was. In Turkey. In the Mediterranean. That mountain over there that towers over Fethiye can probably also be seen from Latoon, a city of ruins lying partially under water. It may even be visible from Xanthos, whose citizens so loved liberty that they twice burned themselves and their town to prevent invaders from capturing it. This may have been the original scorched earth policy. At any rate, the first time they destroyed it, in 540 BC, a disputed number of families were out of town (where? why? no one ever tells us), but when they returned they got right to work and rebuilt the city.

There is nothing like a little history to brighten a swim so I thought some more about all the people before me who might have swum here and I was just getting on to Cleopatra and Anthony and how they ordered sand brought from Egypt to make a beach when Ray called, "We're going to miss our ferry," so I swam to the old pier and climbed out, and we went home and ate watermelon.

It's curtains!

Whenever we told anyone we were taking a year off and going to Turkey we invariably got one of three responses. The first was, "Oh wow, I wish I could do something like that," to which there wasn't much we could say except, "Well, maybe you could."

The second was, "Will you be safe? Aren't you afraid to go there? Didn't you see 'Midnight Express'?" Here we would heave a heavy sigh and say, "Yes," "No," and "No," and wonder if Turkey would ever live down the damage done by that old movie.

The third response was an incredulous, "Really? What are you going to *do* there?" Our usual reply to this was a joyful, "Nothing; we're just going to *be*," which often left our interrogators nonplussed. How could we possibly spend a year doing nothing?

Well we couldn't, of course. But we could spend a year unfettered by the "musts" and "shoulds" that crowded our working lives at home. For one year we were free of the need to earn a living, and early in our stay we discovered we could enjoy activities that back home were simply chores, done without heed on the way to doing something else. Shopping, cooking, and washing dishes became ends in themselves and could be surprisingly pleasant. Our days were filled with supplying basic needs and enjoying simple pleasures: We did the laundry and vacuumed the floors. We read, wrote, and visited. We played with Dodo, Huseyin's dog, and made minor repairs to the apartment. We strolled the promenade, hiked in the hills, swam in the sea, and rode our bicycles everywhere. And when we got bored with Göcek we boarded a bus or rented a car and went someplace else.

Our year without shoulds and musts included an agreement to
avoid until spring the topic of what we would do when our year-
long stay was over—a topic that friends and even just-met acquaintances found irresistible. The harder we tried to avoid it the more
often the question was raised. The truth was we had no plans and
didn't know what we would do, but others found that answer unsat-
isfactory and the query dogged us throughout the year.

August 5

You will cease bemoaning my laziness and inactivity when
you learn that what occupies much of my time these blisteringly hot
days is the crucial work of shifting curtains. Our apartment occupies
the east half of the building, and the sun's first rays shine directly
into the north and east windows of our bedroom. This necessitates,
at sunrise, the first shifting of cream-colored curtains, from open to
closed. On rising a few hours later I see the sun shining through the
office windows and I close those curtains on my way to breakfast.
All the curtains are the same lightweight cotton, and they hang from
wooden rings that make a comforting clunk-clunk sound as they
slide into one another across the round pine poles. About 9 a.m. I
close the curtains on the east side of the living room, followed a few
hours later by those on the southeast side, and finally, in late afternoon I pull the short, single panel across the kitchen's southwest
corner window.

The earth's rotation naturally produces shade on the earlier
sunny windows, and it takes careful watching and exact timing to
reopen curtains that were earlier closed. Sometimes a test opening
reveals a still-sunny ledge and the curtains will need to be redrawn.
You can well imagine that with the added complication of opening

and closing the windows, a conscientious curtain shifter can stay mighty busy.

This exercise is imbued with religious overtones, since the shift-ings often occur during one of the five daily prayer calls that issue from the loudspeaker on the nearby mosque. It also provides an excuse to observe the eucalyptus trees. I've always liked the feathery elegance of these trees, though unless they are grouped tightly their habit of turning leaf edges to the sun means they block little light and are worthless to the shade-seeker. There are lots of eucalyptus here and they dominate the view when we look directly out. Looking down produces quite another picture.

On the northeast side is the "farm," really a large, unorganized garden containing tomatoes, cabbages, beans, eggplants, and more. It is owned by the family who own this apartment building and various family members contribute to its care. The woman we call Grandma is the one we see most often. She marches through the garden at all hours, pounding a stake here, leading the black cow to a new dining location there, or watering or harvesting the mel-ons or tomatoes or beans; always with a cigarette dangling from her lips. She dresses traditionally in a full, gathered print skirt over wide pantaloons, topped by a tee-shirt or sweater. Her hennaed gray braids are tied together at the ends and droop daringly below the traditional white scarf that is twisted precariously atop her head. How she bears this layered costume when it's 95 and humid (and I'm suffering in a tank top and shorts), is beyond my ken.

Further from the house is a stand of corn that is the Baba's do-main (*baba* means father, or head of the household; in this case he's also the *büyükbaba*, or grandpa), and he's often there shifting water hoses around. He's a tall, handsome man with a thick, white, droopy mustache, and he looks quite distinguished when he's dressed for town. It's rumored the Baba "likes the ladies," and it would be no surprise to learn they also like him.

Beyond the corn is a rough dirt road-in-progress, and its creation has brought lots of noise and dust into the apartment. These dirt roads are showing up all over the village, cut at right angles across the fields in a way that reminds us unpleasantly of subdivisions. We hope they are nearly finished, but constant construction is a hallmark of the Turkey we know. Noise, dust, and debris are a given, and one never knows when or where the next project will appear. There are no notices from the city planners here; in fact there are no city planners. The bulldozers and backhoes just show up.

Beyond the road-in-progress is another stand of eucalyptus and to the north are the high, steep, gray rock cliffs that provide a dramatic backdrop to life in Göcek. Looking south the view is not as pleasant—a wide expanse of dirt and gravel leading from the main village road to our building. The hill on the right is where the rock for the road-in-progress comes from, and our view expands as the cliff is gradually and noisily carved away. To the left is the new covered market that is not yet covered. A school is planned for the spot next to the main road, but that will happen long after we've moved on.

Grandma and Grandpa live in an older house behind this one. They are the parents of Yuksel and Mehmet, brothers who run a tourist restaurant in a cove called Deep Bay, about six miles out. Much of the garden's produce is destined for the restaurant, shipped there in Yuksel's old blue and white wooden dinghy.

Yuksel is unmarried; Mehmet and his family live in the one-bedroom apartment just above us. Aygul, his wife, works as a nurse at the hospital in Fethiye, and Grandma takes care of three-year-old

Ipek. I sometimes see Grandma working in the garden with Ipek clinging to her back, held solidly in place with wide, woven straps.

This family might be called transitional, with the grandparents representing the older village values, and the younger generation working to gain a toe-hold in Turkey's growing middle class. In traditional, extended families like this one, income is pooled and everyone, supposedly, works toward a common goal. This age-old arrangement appears to work well and extended families, which may also include aunts, uncles and endless degrees of cousins, rely on one another in all kinds of ways: finding jobs, raising children, working the land, even choosing a mate.

Many of the locals are land rich but cash poor and, like the family who owns our building, they are erecting rentals on their land; new houses and apartments are going up all around us. Our six-unit building will reap benefits for the family as prospective new residents and wealth move into town.

Aygul's job as a nurse takes her away from home during the day, and though we're told nursing is looked down on by some in this country (because, among other things, female nurses touch strange men's bodies, an act disapproved by traditional Moslems) it is a distinct step away from being a peasant farmer, and another indication that women in Turkey are slowly moving out of their traditional sphere into the world of work.

Unlike her mother-in-law, Aygul and her daughter Ipek wear western-style clothes. This is not unusual, but the sight of older women in traditional village garb accompanying daughters and granddaughters clad in the latest Turkish chic, dramatizes the changes underway in Turkish society. These variations in dress are not limited to generational divisions, but reveal class and religious distinctions as well.

I find myself puzzled and fascinated by the Turks' apparent indifference to these differences. I have watched young, conservatively dressed Moslem women in head scarves and full, flowing coats sip tea and share giggles with other young women in tight jeans and midriff-baring tee-shirts, with no obvious tension or even recognition of what appear to me to be glaring differences in their outlook. This tolerance, which is a common Turkish trait, is refreshing, and one of the things I like about the country.

But, I can hear you muttering, what about the intolerance of some conservative Moslems? What about the religious fanatics we hear so much about?

So I must confess that yes, some intolerance does exist. Turkey is not immune from backward or conformist thinking. But acknowledging that minority— which is nowhere evident in this community—I can still say it is pleasant to live amongst such diversity and to enjoy the spirit of cooperation it engenders. And as long as I'm here I'll keep trying to understand how these women live and what these differences mean, if you'll keep trying to remember that I'm really working very hard here, shifting curtains.

Wire tracings

Modern communications make it so easy to stay in touch with home that some of the value of travel is being lost. We both prefer the isolation that comes with having no contact—no telephone, no television, no newspapers or magazines. We want our time away from home to be truly away. Not surprisingly then, to use or not to use email in Turkey occupied our minds for weeks before departure. We didn't want our stay marred by continuous interaction with the west, but email offered quick, frequent, and cheap communication with our daughter, and through her my elderly parents—a major concern. It also allowed us to bypass the unreliable local mail service. In the end we agreed we needed it, and we impetuously promised to send occasional email letters about our experiences to friends and coworkers. It wasn't long before they became a weekly habit.

August 12

It's pretty miraculous that I'm sitting here typing away on a laptop computer in Göcek, Turkey, and you're reading it 9,000 miles away. You would think it even more miraculous if you could see the telephone line this message travels on. To begin with, it's not proper telephone wire, but ordinary black electrical wire—the same kind you find in a cheap extension cord at any hardware store.

The wire leaves our gray plastic Netaş telephone and runs through a hole drilled in the knotty-pine window frame, then sags across the side of the house to our little office balcony, where Ray has fastened it to the back of the railing with thumbtacks so we don't have to look at it. The PTT (Post-Telephone-Telegraph) has been generous and we have lots of extra wire, so at the far end of the balcony about 20 feet of it is wrapped around one of the posts and then coiled down to rest on the red tile floor. It's in the way here, of course, because that corner is where we keep the mop and the broom and the dustpan, and all the empty flower pots that Emma collected, and I'm always kicking it out of the way, or mistakenly trying to set something on it.

From the broom-and-flower-pot corner the wire runs in a long curve up to a third-floor window, where it is caught up with Mehmet and Aygul's telephone wire. Together they loop along the back of the house to yet another window where they are joined by Huseyin's wire, which comes through his living room window (just below our balcony), and muddles about among the cabbages and beans before going up the back wall to the third floor.

The three wires are then tied together in a knot around a couple of rusty nails in the window frame. From there they head out together across the back farm, angling gradually down through the trees toward the grandparent's house, threading their way through the big prickly pear cactus, just high enough to clear the cow's horns, and then into the banana tree. From there the wires disappear into a lower window of the back house and are lost to further examination.

But Türk Telecom is modernizing, even developing an "Internet backbone." When we first came to Turkey ten years ago it was at least a five-year wait to get a telephone line into your house, unless you forked over $500 or so to get a head start. You could do this because people often bought more than one line in order to resell them at a profit. But service has improved; now it only takes a year or two. The wiring has improved too; they are running more than one connection per wire now, so those masses of individual telephone lines, tied together and draped from pole to pole—we've seen bundles 18–24 inches in diameter—are gradually being replaced with the kind of wiring we see at home. Those bundles have an ugly charm about them though, and I'm a little sorry to see them go.

Of course, you don't have to depend on wiring at all. You can use a mobile phone anywhere in Turkey for a quite reasonable rate. At least that's what we hear. Various sources tell us this wonderful cell system was developed by NATO, or by the U.S. government, or by the Turkish army; no one seems to know for sure. But cell phones are extremely popular—at least here on the coast—and its not uncommon to see people gabbing away on the promenade or in a restaurant, just like home. Ray, not wanting to feel left out, bought a toy cell phone at the weekly *pazar*. Push the right button and it rings and says "Numba prease," or "Opa-ator, may I hep you?" in a curiously Chinese voice. It may be that when winter sets in we'll wish we had a real one. If the wind blows that wire any deeper into the prickly pear, we're in trouble.

A certain kind of vowel

There is a great deal of sun along the southwest coast of Turkey, but there is very little under that sun that is new. It is, therefore, not unusual to find foreigners residing in the towns and villages that edge these shores—foreigners have been doing so for centuries beyond recall: soldiers and settlers, saints and scallywags, merchants and travelers. Göcek is no stranger to this tradition and it has a small but varied foreign population. They have come to these shores for reasons as individual as themselves, but always in reference to Turkey's culture, the climate, and the possibility of earning a living. Most are from Great Britain, but we've also met a few Germans, two Dutch, another American, a Canadian, a Romanian, a Russian, and a Thai. Several (women in every case) are married to Turks, and most of the foreigners work. They run restaurants, bars, hotels, *pansiyons*, and retail shops, or they charter yachts or skipper yachts or crew yachts. It is a disparate but interesting group and we've found them welcoming and helpful, willing to answer our endless questions and guide us in the right direction.

A primary attraction for all of us is the friendliness and hospitality of the natives. It is typical of Turks to volunteer their help, and it wasn't surprising when Ziya insisted at our first meeting that we must call her if we needed anything. *"Anything!"*

Ziya, an old friend of Tom and Emma's, had invited them to a farewell lunch and they graciously carried us along with them. She'd prepared an elegant meal that began with paté, included salad, steak (Tom's favorite) and rice pilaf, and ended with Turkey's version of baklava. Though we sat at a shaded outdoor table facing the water, the heat and humidity took the edge off our appetites. Ziya, a petite woman in her mid-forties, chose not to eat. Instead, when she wasn't going to and from the kitchen, she sat at the head of our table smoking and diverting us with conversation laced with an urbane, deadpan humor that was as unexpected as it was entertaining. She has a direct, earnest look, a ready smile, and like most Turks, a quick sense of humor.

A few days later we met again in one of the little grocery stores along the main street, where she was rummaging around in the single, small frozen-food case. We made our way through the formalized Turkish small talk that is always expected here and then in English she said, "Do you shop here often?" We nodded yes and she turned and spoke in Turkish to Ilhan, the son of the shop's owner.

"I told him to give you a discount," she said, turning back to us, "because you are living here now, you should get the Turkish price, not the tourist price."

Ilhan nodded and smiled at us and from that moment, no matter how small our purchase, he would add up the total and say in halting English, "Normal price this much: ____, your price this much: ____."

Down the main street from Ilhan's grocery is the Sevge Bufet, a tiny shop selling beer, wine, and spirits. Aaron, a Turk who lived in Canada for many years, is the owner, and it was he who graciously left his tavla (backgammon) game in the shade and helped Ray with the purchase of our bicycles. The woman who runs the appliance store across the street speaks no English, and our Turkish wasn't up to the intricacies of a bicycle.

Ray writes: *August 18*

They are Hubbys. Or maybe Hibbys, although Karen insists they're Hobbys. The second letter isn't legible, but I suspect it's a vowel. At any rate they are our 18-speed Turkish mountain bikes, normally priced at a cool TL16,000,000 (TL is the monetary designation meaning Turkish Lira, now about TL90,000 to $1 US[1]), but bought at a "very special price" of just 15.5 million each (about $150). Karen's is off-white, mine is candy apple red, and we found them on a rack in front of the household appliance dealer—sort of Coast-to-Coast Stores style.

Almost anyone who knows me is aware that I am a true roadie, having grunted out more than 50,000 miles on my c. 1974 Peugeot PX10. Before I bought my Hubby I had ridden a mountain bike only once for a short distance, "just to get the feel." I was a real road-bike snob, and properly dismounted that sorry excuse in a hurry.

But it didn't take a rocket scientist to see that in Göcek a road bike wouldn't make it. Though the main highway is asphalt, with little or no shoulder, most roads are gravel, or dirt with heavy rock embedded in the surface. The dirt has been ground to a flour-like consistency so the skinny tires of my old Peugeot would sink right in and the heavy rock would pulverize the alloy rims. With no other choice, I took right to my mountain bike, only to find the hills are so steep and rough you can't get traction, even if you could climb them. My record of not having walked a hill since the early 70s went quickly and gracefully by the wayside.

Our Hobbys came equipped with the latest in cycling technology. Certified by Inspektor No. 6, they have a special seat that slides up and down (mostly down), reflectors on the front, back, and in the spokes, Shimano derailleurs, knobby tires, a knock-off wheel, and easy-fill tire valves. My bike came with a special solar-heated bottle, which makes a lot of sense considering the summer's blazing hot days. Affixed to the frame, its black color makes it perfect for keeping one's tea hot. Wire wicker baskets and Turkish glass, blue-eye beads (to keep the evil spirits away) were added as accessories. Whether riding up the dirt track to the spring for ten liters of good-tasting water, bringing home fresh *ekmek* (bread) from the market, going for a swim, or cruising the quay, our Hibbys are just the ticket.

Those of you more technically oriented are undoubtedly wondering what is meant by easy-fill valves. To fill the tires I ride to the *benzene* station at the corner, uncoil the hose from the English Sheffield Automatic Air Pump, pull off the metal apparatus used by motor vehicles, place the open end of the hose over the valve, and let the air flow in. A firm squeeze on the tire lets me know precisely when the desired pressure is attained.

If I get a flat tire I go to "Bicycle Repair" (patching kits don't seem to exist) located on the main highway west of the borek stand. The boy in the lean-to shack, who looks to be a competent twelve years of age, locates the puncture and places a vulcanizing patch over it. He then asks if I have a match and finding that I don't, skillfully ignites the patch with his arc-welding torch. The repair being complete, TL100,000 changes hands, and I'm off again on my Hobby for yet another adventure.

Desperately seeking yag

Ray writes: *August 26*

After we purchased our mountain bikes I thought it would be nice to have a small can of oil in order to lubricate them. Besides, we had some squeaky cabinet doors that needed silencing. The appliance shop where we purchased our bikes (they also sell clothes washers) doesn't carry oil. If this store doesn't carry it, surely the hardware store will.

I looked up the word in our dictionary. Yag. It's pronounced "yaaaw." After carefully making a diagram of an oil can in my ever present notebook, pronouncing the word several times using Karen as my critic, and writing the word down in Turkish, I headed confidently to the hardware shop. Greeting the clerk with my best Turkish hello, I looked for yag. Not finding it (maybe it's in the back?) I presented my diagram and boldly said, "yaaaw."

He looked at me with grave skepticism, then looked at my drawing and told me he didn't carry oil, that I should try the oil shop. After receiving his directions I headed down the main street to the square and found the oil shop just behind the butcher shop. I entered and asked the lad if he had oil in a small can.

"Sit down please," he said. "You like something to drink?" His English was little better than my Turkish. Since it was blazing hot outside I asked for *su* (water) and he sent his young apprentice out to get some. I think it would have been better to ask for tea. It's much easier to find.

"Why you want oil for?"

"My bicycle," I answered.

"Where is it?"

I went around the building, got my bicycle, and wheeled it back for him to see.

"Did you rent it?" We keep no secrets here.

"New, doesn't need oil," he said after looking it over. Then for the next hour and a half I watched as he checked and tightened virtually every nut and bolt. It seems that bicycle Inspektor No. 6 must have had a sore wrist the day my bicycle was assembled. I hope the inspektor has recovered.

While he was working on my bicycle and I was drinking my *su*, an old man who spoke no English cajoled me into playing a game of dominos with him. Being the gracious host that Turks are, he lost, calling me "Champion." Then he kindly offered me my own set for a mere TL500,000.

After the bicycle was tightened properly, I learned that the oil store doesn't carry small containers of oil, only big ones for yachts.

After hunting in vain in several other shops, I turned my attention to the open-air market. No oil to be found. After two more weeks of fruitless searching our next-door neighbor alerted me that he had seen oil in the market at a tool vendor's stall. Needless to say I rushed right down, finding the tool vendor but no yag. Imagine how crushed I was. But I decided to ask anyway and he looked in the back of his station wagon and, like a magician, pulled a plastic container from a small white bag.

"This Singer (pronounced sing-grrr) oil, very good quality," and it was priced at only 150,000 TL. So after three weeks of searching, I have my yag. The cabinet doors, which I had temporarily silenced with olive oil, don't squeak anymore, and my bicycle hums like a sewing machine.

Lost in Fethiye

September 2

 The two teenage boys in the seat ahead of us have been giggling ever since we left Göcek. They are 15 or 16 years old and look immature by American standards, but not so immature that they don't nearly break their necks to goggle at every young woman along the roadside. We are bouncing along the highway in a *dolmuş* on our way to Fethiye, at 10 a.m. in the morning. This Peugeot van, which seats 14, is full but *dolmuş* means stuffed and we're barely out of town before we halt to pick up two more passengers, a stooped, toothless old man and a young woman who must be his daughter. Since custom decrees that women and men who don't know one another should not sit side by side, and since these bench seats hold four people across (and we're squeezing five), there is some good-humored shifting to accommodate this unspoken rule.

 Dolmuses are the bottom rung of an excellent bus system in Turkey, and since we have no car they're our major means of traveling beyond the village. These little buses put the U.S. public transportation system—or what remains of it—to shame. Now, during the tourist months of May through October, this *dolmuş* runs back and forth between Göcek and Fethiye every hour, all day, every day. It's a 40-minute trip that costs about $1.20. There's hardly a village in the country that you can't get to by *dolmuş*, though you may only be able to go there once a day.

 There's a lot of conversation among our passengers, including the two gigglers who are talking with a chattering, dark-haired girl of about 20. She's been talking nonstop ever since she reached the bus stop in Göcek, with only a slight pause as she slipped into English to offer us a seat, "no problem." It's not unusual to hear bantering and conversation on these little buses: neighbors know neighbors here, and riding a *dolmuş* is a common experience; private cars are still a luxury.

This is our second trip to the big city (pop. 35,000); the first was on a midibus that we caught by walking up to the highway and flagging it down. Midibuses are the next leg up in the system, and this time of year one seldom has to wait more than 15 minutes for a ride. They run on regular and frequent schedules and there's a lot of competition for customers. The midis carry about 25 passengers and an attendant and driver. If you're very lucky the air conditioning will work, and the radio and tape deck certainly will. The Turks are a fastidious people and the buses and vans we've ridden have been remarkably clean inside and out. It's not unusual, on a longer ride, to find your bus pulling into a service station for a quick soaping and scrub down.

There seem to be local, regional and national bus companies, both publicly and privately owned, and the midis and the *dolmuses* and the cross-country big-buses all meet up at the *otogar*.

Otogars, or bus stations, come in various sizes and offer various services, depending on the size of the town. Göcek's *otogar* consists of a small shed hugging one corner of the village parking lot, with a few of those ubiquitous white plastic chairs scattered around. Ostensibly the chairs are for waiting passengers, but in fact they are usually filled by drivers waiting to take the next trip out, or friends of the drivers, or passers-by looking for a glass of tea or a friendly game of tavla. The Turks are good hosts though, and always willing to relinquish a chair to a waiting customer.

The Fethiye *otogar* is typical of larger towns. Covering nearly an acre of asphalt and concrete, it has a covered perimeter with a few scattered tables and more white plastic chairs, a couple of buffets selling soft drinks and ice cream, toilets (pretty clean), a newsstand, and a barber. Larger stations also have shops selling "fast" food, like *pide* (Turkish pizza), *doner kabob* sandwiches (usually lamb, sometimes chicken), and pastries.

There are always drivers or touts about, and during the busy tourist months the air is alive with their shouts as they hawk the company's service and line up customers for the next trip out. These men—they're always men—are helpful; if they're not going where you want to go, they're happy to direct you to the right place. But of course you have to know where you are going.

Since this is our first *dolmuş* ride into Fethiye we're not sure where to get off, though we were given directions by our friendly local *bufet* owner.

"At the hospital," he said. But when Ray spots a sign to the city "centrum" and thinks the bus is going to turn in the opposite direction he says,

"This is it."

"Are you sure? I don't think this looks like the hospital."

"Yes, come on" he says, signaling the driver to stop.

So being a dutiful wife I follow him off the van.

Need I say this is not the right place? Never mind. The driver and all the passengers also know it, so when we walk around the corner toward town we see the *dolmuş* parked at the curb and the driver standing in back, motioning us aboard. We sheepishly climb back into our seats to the sound of good-natured laughter. Two kilometers further on we get off in front of the hospital.

Turkey's in the news

Early in our stay several events occurred that caused friends at home to question our safety. In addition to the continuing dispute with the Kurds of eastern Turkey there were clashes with the Greeks. A tiny, uninhabited island off Turkey's west coast was the focus of potential violence when Turkish and Greek flags were alternately raised over it by enthusiastic nationalists. Gunboats patrolled, tensions ran high, and American negotiators stepped in. Shortly after that Cyprus came once more to the world's attention when both Greeks and Turks there were killed.

These events did not go unnoticed in Göcek, but we heard little animosity expressed toward the Greeks. Most of the Turks we knew decried the violence, and referred to both incidents as "just politics."

September 6

As observers who speak neither Turkish nor Greek it's impossible to comment authoritatively on the events in Cyprus and the disputed islands and we don't intend to try. The long history between these two lands, of attacks and counterattacks, invasions and occupations, extends back in time to before the invasion of Troy, and it's beyond our meager power to make sense of it.

Superficially there are many similarities between the two countries. The same rugged, gray, dry mountains rim the Aegean Sea that they share, and the same olive-covered terraces grace both shores. Their houses are built using the same construction methods and materials and they often look identical. Their folk music and musical instruments sound remarkably similar to our uneducated ears, though we're told they would dispute that. Their national drinks, raki and ouzo, are two sides of the same coin, and many of their favorite dishes are similar. The ruins scattered across mainland Greece and her rocky Aegean islands also extend far into the interior of Turkey and have a common source and a common history. Despite all this, or because of it, there is conflict.

We don't see that conflict here in Göcek, any more than we don't see the Turkish government's human rights abuses, or the Kurdish fighters playing seek and shoot with Turkish troops and other Kurds. We are as isolated from it here as we were at home in the U.S.

Turkey will be our home for the next ten months, however, and there's no doubt that, try as we might for objectivity, we will see the events surrounding us from a Turkish point of view. It was easy for us decry the abuses reported on America's front pages. It's less easy here, where we are reminded every day that Turkey is a young republic surrounded by unfriendly governments with churning ethnic and economic problems: Iraq, Iran, Syria (and beyond them Jordan, Lebanon, Israel, and Egypt), Georgia, Armenia, Bulgaria and the Balkans, and Greece. Seventy years ago the Anatolian peninsula was ruled by a corrupt and failing Ottoman Empire. Today it's walking the tightrope of economic development vs. religious fervor, led by a divided government with an immature infra-structure. From where we sit now—human rights abuses excepted—it's doing a reasonable job.

Can the Çan live up to its billing?

September 9

Unable to break the habit of work and deadlines, and wanting to stay in touch with friends at home who didn't have email, we decided to produce and mail a six-page newsletter, the *Göcek Gazette*. Our original intent was to do three issues during our year-long stay, but as the habit of work waned, so did our desire to meet deadlines, and in the end we produced only one and a half issues, and the half never got mailed. The following piece was a restaurant review in the first issue:

The Çan (pronounced Jahn) was the site of a recent dinner outing by your reporters, who remained dutifully anonymous. Choosing a table under the grape arbor facing the sea, we began by ordering a half serving of raki, Turkey's national drink. The waiter, a charming and handsome young man from the provinces (all waiters can be so described) returned promptly with a small pitcher, an ice bucket and two glasses, along with a basket of toast and a generous portion of herb butter. At this point your reporters nearly forgot their purpose, so engrossed were they in enjoying the aniseed liquor and the sumptuous bread and butter.

However, after a few desultory comments about the heat, the appearance of a familiar dog, the good behavior of Turkish children, and the gross size of an incoming yacht, we returned to business and moved to the refrigerated display case to order our mezes. (Mezes are "starters" but are usually more filling than hors d'oeuvres. There seem to be an infinite variety of these dishes.)

We chose a dish of minced vegetables: eggplant, potatoes, onions, tomatoes and garlic; green peppers stuffed with a mixture of rice, pine nuts and currants; borek stuffed with cheese and nettles, and cucumbers and garlic in yogurt. We passed over the zucchini fritters, the black pasta (made with octopus ink), and the potato croquettes, only because we thought it prudent to save room for the main course.

Within a few minutes the CHYMFP delivered our dishes and we set to work, painstakingly analyzing for your benefit the relative merit of each. After topping off our raki, and with suitable deliberation, we reached unanimous agreement—all were delicious. Bravo Çan!

At this point a break in the proceedings was called for and your reporters had a pleasant discussion on the relative merit of cats versus dogs in restaurants, the curiousness of nut, mussel, and cotton-candy vendors wandering through restaurants selling their wares, and the pleasantness of the breeze which was finally making an appearance. We then returned to the display case to choose our entree and it was here that we realized we had made a dreadful error. The case was full of seafood. We have nothing against seafood, mind you, but it is always expensive and by this time we had so overindulged on mezes we were reluctant to order a costly dish we knew we couldn't finish. We therefore chose the cheaper but still appealing chicken shish and grilled chicken, much to the CHYMFP's disdain.

A short wait provided an opportunity to reappraise the raki, but all too soon dinner was served and we were back again at work.

Lo and behold, the chicken was tender and well seasoned, the potatoes fried in olive oil were light and flavorful, the tomatoes were sweet and juicy, the rice pilaf was . . . too much. We reluctantly put down our forks and fed the remainder to the cats.

No dinner in Turkey is really complete without coffee, however, so the male member of your reporting team bravely ordered *kahve sade* (Turkish coffee without sugar). The CHYMFP was again delighted with us—we had proven we were no slouches after all and knew what a dinner was for. He returned flourishing the coffee and a complimentary serving of melon that we were almost able to finish. All in all a delightful culinary experience.

Street food in Istanbul

FALL

It must be fall

September 16

He is six or seven years old and he's being measured for his new school uniform. Standing with his weight on one hip, the opposite foot angled smartly out, he struggles to maintain an expression of bored indifference, but his secret delight can't be hidden and no one is fooled. Two women are eyeing him severely and discussing sizes, and all around us in Göcek's bustling Sunday market hang the blue shirts and dresses of Turkey's national school uniform. It must be fall.

Over in the veggie stalls, where fall's cabbages and apples have replaced summer's cherries and honeydews, we greet Hakan, the thirteen-year-old boy we visit with nearly every week. His English, learned, "at my school in Dalaman," is remarkably good. He and Ray became buddies the first or second week we were here, after Ray asked him if he knew where Oregon was.

"No," he said (and of course he's not alone).

"Well, if you can tell me where it is when I see you next week," said Ray, "I'll give you a souvenir from there."

"Canada," he said confidently on the following Sunday, "and there are lots of mountains and big trees there." Close enough, we figure, for someone who probably doesn't have access to a map. He was delighted with his Oregon patch, and Ray has a friend for the duration.

The blue uniforms and the good English are proof that education has come a long way since 1924 when Atatürk, the founder of modern Turkey, closed the Ottoman religious schools and made elementary school attendance compulsory. No public school infrastructure existed in 1924, but according to my U.S. government handbook on Turkey, the 1990 overall literacy rate was 81 percent (90 percent among adult males, and 71 percent among females). There are five stages of public school education here: preschool, primary, middle, high school, and university. The five-year primary and two-year middle school is compulsory, but officials often do not enforce the middle-school requirement, especially for girls and in villages where schools may be distant. Many children attend Moslem religious schools instead of the state-sponsored middle schools, and officials in government and business express concern over this growing phenomenon.[2]

There are 1,300 public high schools in the country, divided into lycees (general) and vocational schools. With the exception of some vocational schools, all are co-educational. The largest cities have lycees that are bilingual, teaching classes in Turkish and either English, German, or French. (The English school our young friend attends in a small town nearby is a private one, funded by one of Turkey's influential families.)

Like many countries with nervous governments, Turkey has some rigid rules regarding education, and some of our acquaintances here criticize what they see as a lack of imagination in teaching, and the emphasis on rote learning. Beverly, a former grade-school teacher in the U.S. tells us about an eight-year-old Turkish child she was tutoring in English who—when given blank paper and crayons—consistently could not draw a picture until Beverly drew one first for the child to copy. Libraries, we're told, are poor or nonexistent and reading is not encouraged.

Much of the control, however, comes at the university level, where the government has the power to appoint university rectors, and prohibits students and faculty from belonging to, or working for, political parties. It also requires a standardized university curriculum. Testing occurs at each level of advancement, and since here, as in the U.S., education facilitates upward mobility, there are consistently more applicants than spaces. This emphasis on competition and testing has many parents and educators feeling frustrated, and rumors of possible changes in the system have surfaced frequently since our arrival.

There are few private universities. Bilkent University in Ankara is the oldest, and in a report on the 10th anniversary of its founding the *Turkish Daily News* waxed eloquent:

"The single most striking evidence of the high level of instruction in the university is the outstanding results obtained by Bilkent engineering students in the Graduate Record Examination (GRE). . . . Students who took the GRE in 1995 ranked first among the top 25 engineering schools in the United States and their average analytical score was in the top 10. To put the matter simply, Bilkent faculty of engineering equals in academic excellence, if not surpasses, its counterparts in internationally renowned universities such as Harvard, Caltech [sic], MIT, Stanford and Carnegie Mellon."

Bilkent University has 10,000 students studying in seven faculties, or departments. Twenty percent of undergraduates and most graduate students are on full scholarship. In 1995 Bilkent spent $2.2 million for the acquisition of books, journals and CDs, and the library's collection, which is open to the public, expands by 23,000 to 30,000 books a year. (Historian Norman Stone, in a 1997 article in *Cornucopia* magazine states Bilkent University's library "buys as many books in a year as fifty British ones.") The university can do this because it wholly owns 30 profitable companies, from construction, to furniture, to tourism, and all profits go to the institute.

I guess that means that, being tourists, we can pat ourselves on the back. During three visits over ten years at least some of our tourism dollars may have gone to Bilkent University. With luck maybe one of the boys in the market will make it there too.

Market women in Bodrum

What we did today

September 22

Deciding to go to Turkey was easy, in part, because we had friends there. Rick and Beverly shared many of our interests, including a love of travel and the belief that simplicity was better than abundance. We liked them immensely. Rick's sense of humor often edged into corniness, but he could always make me laugh and I loved him for it. Beverly was smart, fun, and full of curiosity. She was also amazingly tough. They had come to Turkey ten years ago, agreeing they would try it for one year. Within a few weeks they had found the perfect flat overlooking Bodrum's crusader castle and the sea and there they had remained. For the first eight years they were without a phone; they still had no car and no TV, but they could claim a large circle of friends. They had adapted well to the country's sometimes quirky and unfathomable culture. Unlike we two drifters Rick and Beverly appeared fully in charge of their lives. For many reasons, we had a great deal of respect for them.

Beverly first passed through our lives briefly in the early 70s, but we lost track of her after she divorced and moved to Thailand to teach in an international elementary school. There she met Rick, a divorced Air Force captain with two young daughters. Rick and Beverly married and shortly after were transferred to the Philippines. It was there, a year later, that a plane carrying Beverly and her mother and sister on a sightseeing flight crashed in the jungle and Beverly's back was broken.

The anguish, pain, and frustration such an event calls forth may be taken as a given. Beverly was paralyzed from the waist down, and began life again in a wheelchair. They moved to Texas where, searching for an activity they could enjoy as a family, they discovered sailing. This they so loved that when Rick completed 20 years in the military he chose retirement and he and Beverly left their now-grown daughters behind and moved to Turkey, where the cost of living was low and the sailing near perfect. It was there in 1987 that, through a mutual friend, we found Beverly again and rekindled our friendship. And it was Beverly who sent the fax that had brought us to Turkey:

"Some English friends are renting their apartment, furnished, for a year or more," she wrote. "It's in a small village on the coast, a few hours from here. Please come. We think you would like it."

It was their idea to meet us on the Greek island of Kos and carry us to Bodrum, Turkey in their yacht, the 38-foot, steel-hulled *Livonia*, and we agreed the 12-mile sail would be a perfect way to start the year. When we climbed down from the airport bus in Kos Town and wearily tugged our bags down to the harbor we found *Livonia* tied up under the old castle walls, right where they'd promised she would be. A handmade canvas banner reading, "Ray and Karen—free at last!" was draped across the stern and a portable tape deck piped us aboard to the tune of "Stars and Stripes Forever."

It was clear from the beginning that our friends hoped we would love Turkey as much as they did and stay permanently, and we had long conversations about the pros and cons of doing this. Turkey was inexpensive, scenic, interesting, full of friendly people, and people who were friends. But it was also a long, expensive flight home, and we had family there who depended on us.

In the Fall our friends sailed *Livonia* around the Datça peninsula and into Fethiye Bay for a three-week stay. We'd been eagerly anticipating their visit: time for conversation, for sailing, for shopping in Göcek's little boutiques, and for entertaining them in our home for a change.

Their arrival was punctuated with questions: how did we like the apartment? Was Turkey as we remembered? How we were spending our time? Had I done any writing? Had we made any friends? What did we think of Göcek? And that dreaded query, what would we do when our year here was over? We could answer all but the last. There, we declared, we had no answer. Like Scarlett, we would think about it tomorrow, and tomorrow had been assigned to the following March. We were still getting used to the present. One day, joking with them about how we filled our new-found time (and wondering ourselves) we sat down and wrote the following.

Ray writes: Woke up at 6:20 a.m. and fixed myself a cup of coffee. Did some computer accounting until 7 a.m. when I tuned in BBC shortwave news from London. Plugged stock market and currency data into my Excel spreadsheets and played a couple games of computer backgammon. Greeted Karen when she awoke at 8 a.m. Slung my camera over my shoulder and rode my Hubby out to the highway to check out the colorful Turkish trucks as they drove toward me into the sunlight. Clouds moved in (no photos) so I rode back to the village along the quay and heard Rick call to me across the harbor. Rode over to *Livonia*, climbed into the cockpit, had another cup of coffee, heard about their starter-motor problems and discussed Middle East news. When the electrician arrived I bicycled back to the apartment and met Karen at around 9:30 a.m.

Karen writes: Got up about 8, had coffee with Ray (thanks Ray), cursed because the water was off, said good-bye to Ray, had my second cup of coffee with the BBC. Water magically returned so showered, dressed, made bed and did last night's dinner dishes. Ray returned from ride, showered and shaved, and we climbed on our bikes and rode to the village to look for a blanket (it's starting to get cool at night, a sheet no longer does it). Went to the soft-goods-and-yacht-sewing-store, asked about blankets, decided we didn't like the only one they had (lavender), rode to the ATM machine and got five million (!) in cash, rode back to retrieve a necklace that had been left for repair.

Greeted two acquaintances on their way to catch the ferry to Club Marina, sat down with another and had tea. Talked for an hour. Sat guard in a shop while owner took Ray to find out about homemade butter and yogurt (thank goodness no one came in). Stayed another 15 minutes, then rode over to *Livonia* and met Rick on his way back to the electrician (I have learned this about boats: there is always something wrong with something). Rick borrowed my bike and Ray and I climbed aboard and drank a diet Coke with Beverly while we talked about boats, cars, and Afghanistan. Rick returned with electrician in tow so we climbed back aboard bikes and rode home.

Ray writes: After late-lunching on tuna salad sandwiches I tried unsuccessfully to nap. Then I fixed the roof on Dodo's dog house (Dodo belongs to our downstairs neighbor), swept the stairs, retrieved a fax from friends in England, did some reading and writing, split a beer with Karen, and prepared dinner while listening to the Voice of America (VOA) middle-east edition of the news.

Karen writes: After late-lunching on tuna salad sandwiches I collected yesterday's laundry off the clothesline and put it away, then sat on the deck and read a chapter in Will Durant's *The Life of Greece*. Got up and filed my nails, sat at the computer and tried unsuccessfully to write, returned to book. Ray got up from nap and we had a cup of tea and split a perfect peach and talked. I then looked for a recipe—unsuccessfully. Found a thick picture book about kitchens (1977) and sat on the "settee" and looked at pictures and drank my half beer while Ray fixed spaghetti for dinner. Book told of easy way to clean copper: add salt to vinegar and rub lightly. Tried it on one of Emma's thousand pieces of copper and, gloriosky, it works.

We then took turns writing this account, I did the dishes while listening to Ella Fitzgerald, and after such an exhausting day it's time to say goodnight.

A creek without a paddle

"Along the tracks our drivers stoop to pick up numerous very tiny stones the color of turquoise, which seem dazzling on the dirty gray of the ground. These are pieces of the beads that usually adorn camels' heads. From time immemorial these same paths have been used by caravans, so the fashion of this jewelry must go back three to four thousand years. The pieces of glass beads that we are collecting and that seem to be polished fossils could easily go back to the time of Moses or Solomon. It is strange to see these small, blue, almost eternal things that fell one by one over the years, finally marking the trail on these endless paths like Tom Thumb's crumbs of bread."

That is Pierre Loti writing in *The Desert,* a beautiful, poetic book about crossing the Sinai desert in 1894. I was delighted to find this passage because the blue beads of which he writes are ubiquitous here in Turkey, and their origin has been a minor mystery to us—one of those puzzles that travelers so often come across. Sometimes, surrounded by the modern, touristy accoutrements of the Mediterranean coast, I forget that Turkey belongs more to the east than the west. The beads are a visible remnant of its ties to other equally old and superstitious cultures.

We see turquoise beads everywhere: decorating the woven camel straps we buy as souvenirs, sewn into pillow covers and saddle bags and purses, worn as amulets on elegant gold bracelets and necklaces, or as rings or earrings, and clustered in the baskets and bins that hug the doors of tourist shops. Most are fashioned to resemble eyes, for their primary function is to protect the bearer from the dangers of the "evil eye." Small children go off to school guarded by tiny blue-eyed beads pinned to their clothing with safety pins, and no matter how modern or sophisticated a Turk may be, the blue bead of protection is always nearby. (The same blue beads are sold in Greece, for the same purpose.)

Doorways are vulnerable to evil eye manifestations and rare is the entrance that doesn't display a large eye nearby; even new, modern high rises are well protected. Naturally, our apartment has one prominently displayed above the entrance.

September 28

Our English neighbors Bob and Helen appeared on our doorstep not long ago and since the big blue glass bead above the door didn't crash and break (a sure sign that the evil eye has been turned on us), we let them in. Helen is Tom's sister (Tom, in case you've forgotten, is our landlord) and she and Bob keep a sailboat in Göcek and an apartment in this building. I was apprehensive about their arrival because Helen is responsible for our apartment in Tom's absence, and I wondered how it would be having an overprotective "landlord" hovering twelve feet away.

My fears were groundless, however, for our new neighbors are low-keyed, friendly, and good-humored. They've given us valuable insights into our Turkish neighbors, and have introduced us to yet more people in Göcek. Like a lot of expats who spend most of their time sailing, they have seen little of Turkey's interior and it didn't take long to decide that our common lack of knowledge could be a source of mutual enjoyment. To that end we rented a car for a day and the four of us set out.

Our route took us first to Hursur Vadasi (Peaceful Valley) a place tucked into the high mountains behind Göcek. This is an unusual little resort, now in its second season, where visitors sleep in traditional nomads' yurts, painstakingly handmade of heavy wool felt over bent, interlaced branches. Inside, the yurts are surprisingly roomy and they have that wonderful feeling of expansiveness that circular, domed buildings always convey. And like the traditional yurts that inspired them, they're decorated with the multicolored rugs and hangings that are so plentiful here.

Bob and Helen had brought us here to meet the owners, but two were away and the other was asleep, having put in a long night at the airport waiting for guests. In lieu of the owners we spent a pleasant hour drinking tea and visiting with a Welsh couple, teachers of Tai Chi, who praised the quiet ambiance and the excellent cooking.

Making our way back down the dusty dirt road we regain the highway and follow the signs past Fethiye to a secondary road that climbs up and up again through pine forests to a little-known ruin. High on a mountain top, with the sea glimpsed far, far away, are the buried remains of a city dating back to the 5th century B.C. —Kadyanda. The site is largely untouched; it has only recently been opened to the public and there is no apparent excavation being done. A path thick and soft with pine needles wanders from one mound to another, but here are some ruined marble steps, the tiered seats of a stadium, and—look out!—dangerous drops into deep cisterns, where the unwary could easily tumble. The trail takes us in a long circle around the ruins, perhaps a mile or more through sparse pine trees and low shrubs, and I find myself drawn by imagination into that ancient world. Helen, I find, shares my love of uncovered, unreconstructed sites, and we pause now and then to speculate on what lies below the stony hillocks at our feet.

It's mid-afternoon when we finally leave, and hunger is up-permost in our minds. We head south, toward the ruins of Xanthos, hoping to find a restaurant on the way. Fortunately one never has to travel far in Turkey to find food, and at a crossroads we spot tables under tall deciduous trees and see the rotund owner, anxious for cus-tomers, eagerly waving us in. It's nearly 90°F with matching humid-ity and the shady tables look inviting. Any food will do, we agree, as we pile out of the little car.

We can't agree, though, on where to sit. We wander from table to table, looking for the coolest possible spot. Typical square, plas-tic tables stand under shady branches, their typical, colorful cloths flapping in the slight, hot breeze. It's not until we sit down near a low stone wall that we discover the restaurant's true specialty. Look-ing over the wall, Helen points dramatically and declares, "There's where we can sit!"

The four of us peer over the wall to see five white plastic tables sitting serenely in a running brook. Two of the tables have diners around them, happily munching while soaking their bare feet in eight or ten inches of cool, burbling water. Nothing could be more appealing on this hot day. We signal to our waiter and follow Bob past the stone building that houses the kitchen and down a short flight of stairs, where we quickly shed our shoes and step into the creek.

Ahhh, cool! Ahhh, bliss!

Stepping easily out of his rubber flip-flops the waiter follows us into the creek, carrying a red plastic crate that he places under the table—to rest our feet on should they grow too cold. We order four Efes beers, mixed salad, chips, and lamb kebabs, and sit back to enjoy the cool, shady vista. No, we agree, none of us has ever eaten in a creek before.

Our delight at finding this place equals our delight at finding new friends, for it's clear by this time we enjoy one another's company. We linger over our late lunch and by the time Ray pulls out his camera for a final photo the sun has started its downward slide. Reluctantly, we pay the bill, pull our sandals back on, and say goodbye to the creek. Shaking hands with the waiter—a very Turkish custom—we climb back into the dusty car and drive off toward the ruins of Xanthos, blessing the still-long days that allow us one more stop.

Roadside friends

Tea and the weaver's art

September 30

They are many and multihued and they lay in high, folded stacks along three sides of the room. They hang, like supple stained glass, from the walls and rafters, they drape over chairs and chests, they spread in tangled heaps across the floor. Their patterns, geometric and intricate, dance across the plush surfaces and vibrate with an almost tangible warmth. They are handmade Turkish carpets, and like every traveler who has ever crossed the threshold of such a shop, we are enthralled. Crossing that threshold can have alarming repercussions though, and since this is our third trip to Turkey you'd think we would know better. Still, what better way to spend an evening in Antalya?

We've only stopped in for a moment though, to be polite; we're not buying. (We've told ourselves this very firmly.) The young salesman who helped us find our *pansiyon* works here, and we came to say thank you. Well, yes, of course we'll have tea.

This is a favorite tactic of Turkish salesmen, helping you out and then inviting you in for tea. But it's not totally self-serving. The Turks are genuinely helpful, and tea is just tea. One is never obliged to buy, and if one lacks will power when faced with hundreds of irresistible works of art, it's not the salesman's fault is it?

No. So here we are, surrounded by rippling color, seated on a long rug- and cushion-covered bench, sipping tea and talking about everything but carpets. The young Samaritan has introduced us to one of the shop's owners, a man only slightly older, clad in a black leather jacket and speaking English like a native. He's interesting and articulate, not pushy, and we sip tea and talk for 30 minutes before the subject of carpets is raised. This is part of the game. I'm surprised when Ray agrees to look at some, but since we've nothing but dinner planned for the evening, why not?

Shopping for carpets in Turkey should be a slow, almost languorous process, and as Westerners we're at a disadvantage. We don't appreciate the choreographed moves, the formalized courtesies, the give and take of a long negotiation. Nevertheless, I'm content to sit and drink tea and watch as rug after rug is pulled from the stacks, spread out to view, tossed carelessly to one side and replaced by another. Since looking was Ray's idea I'm keeping my mouth shut, but I begin to wonder how he will extricate himself from this mesmerizing display.

While he is pacing around the carpets that are now fanned out three deep in front of us, I watch a German family who have just entered. They are not in a languorous mood. They sit uncomfortably on the edge of the carpet-covered bench, like canaries perched for flight. The salesman, who has caught their mood, stands behind a folded pile of mediocre-looking kilims, briskly holding up one after another and stating the price while the woman, who's a bit cross, passes judgment on each. The rugs fall to one side or the other, into yea or nay piles. It's all business, and quick business at that. When the bottom of the stack is reached they start again on the yea pile. And then, as quickly as they arrived, they're gone. Did they buy? If so I missed it. All that's left is a tossed pile of kilims being refolded by a bored young assistant.

In the meantime Ray has gotten more and more drawn in, he's now looking at kilims too, his weakness. While I've been daydreaming he's narrowed his selection down to four or five, and we've entered the danger zone. I begin to think he's actually going to buy something, and decide to offer an out.

"Shall we go and have dinner?" I say. "We can come back later if you want."

He ignores my escape gambit and instead embarks on a long conversation about sales techniques. I get up and move over to the kilims. There are several that he likes but he's focused on an old one. The Samaritan, seeing me finally show some interest, starts telling me about it, a kilim made for a woman's dowry but never used. Since nearly every carpet and kilim and sumak is beautiful in my eyes he's wasting his time. I would buy them all if I could. Deciding to see if Ray is really serious, I offer a second opportunity for escape.

"You know Ray, we're going to be in town again next week. We could come back then, after we've had time to think about them."

He ignores that too. Well, okay. I'm game. I guess we're buying.

By this time our wily salesman has us pegged. He knows what we like and he brings out another one. Now the negotiating begins.

One for this price, but two at this.

No, this one only, this price.

Well, this price, but see here, this is better, two for this price.

I am now on my third glass of tea, and we've been here nearly three hours. The offers fly back and forth, the merits of this kilim or that one fill the air, and at one point we break into giggles remembering that at present we haven't got a home to put any kilim in. At last, though, the deed is done. The kilims are wrapped, payment is made, and we, the knowing, determined, nonbuying buyers depart, leaving the knowing, determined seller smiling at his doorstep, inviting us to come back, anytime. We got the better of him though. We got an evening's entertainment and two wonderful pieces of the traditional weaver's art. He only got money.

A rug salesman

A working woman

October 6

Every morning we watch a woman go to work. Her habits are typical of workers everywhere: she dresses to suit the occasion, goes back and forth at regular hours, and carries some of her work with her. She passes the house about 9 a.m., on her way to where I cannot say. Her work clothes consist of an ankle-length calico-print skirt and blouse over differently-patterned pantaloons. Around her head she wraps a white scarf edged with colorful crocheted flowers, and on her feet she wears the rubber, open-toed sandals that every Turk loves.

She walks with a stoop because a huge load of freshly cut branches rests on her back, and the greenery sways and bounces as she moves. With her are a varying number of goats; black, white, and brown. Several of the goats are young, and they hop around, playfully butting one another as they follow. They are not roped together and she does not pay them much heed, but they follow. She is heading toward the village, but she must veer off before she gets there because the village is not a good place for a heavily laden woman with five goats. The village has yachts, and tourists wearing halter tops and platform shoes, and lots of busy little shops that are open at least an hour before the woman crosses our view each morning.

Some of the shop owners live in Göcek year round; others live elsewhere—Ankara or Istanbul maybe—and come here for the tourist season. All of them keep long hours. The stores open at 8 a.m. and close at midnight, or later. If they're lucky the owners have spouses, brothers, fathers, sisters, or cousins to help. A few of them hire assistants (often young teens), but most businesses are family-run and the owners are usually present throughout the long day, seven days a week, from April through October. The few shops that stay open through the winter look forward to closing at 5 p.m. after the season ends.

Perhaps because they work such long hours, people here take a more relaxed view of business than is expected of U.S. workers. Many stores have TVs to help fill the time (yesterday in the grocery the Flintstones was playing, today it was Clint Eastwood). Nearly all have chairs outside where the owners/employees can sit and pass the time of day with their neighbors or customers over a cup of tea; there is always much visiting back and forth, and good-natured ribbing and laughter are not infrequent since a good sense of humor is thought by Turks to be a sign of intelligence.

All these people have become familiar faces to us now, as we have to them. Sometimes during the short walk from one end of the village street to the other we are brought to a halt four or five times, to exchange greetings and small talk. Like small towns everywhere, this one is full of gossip and complaints, and plans and dreams. This person is planning a bigger store next year; that one is giving up altogether. One complains of the long hours; another looks forward to visiting her mother in Istanbul when the season ends.

Last night we had dinner with two shop owners, Yusuf and Carol. Yusuf sells those wonderful Turkish carpets and Carol, his wife, sells pottery, Uzbek embroidery, and other exotic goods. We sat in a restaurant across from her shop and she kept a casual eye on it through dinner, leaving us once to wait on a customer. After dinner Yusuf returned to his shop and we walked over and sat with Carol until 11:30 p.m.. We talked about kilims, and pottery, and life in Turkey, and watched with morbid fascination as the doctor, whose office is next door, hunched into the back of a battered station wagon to examine a young woman brought from a distant village. She had been bitten in the neck by a snake hidden in the hayloft of the family barn, and when at last he pronounced her dead, friends and curious onlookers rushed to console the family, while the doctor closed the car's rear door and sadly shook his head.

"He takes it personally," Carol said, "because he knows everyone in the area and most likely has taken care of them."

The doctor probably knows the woman with the goats as well, and maybe he knew her mother or even her grandmother. Those women probably kept goats too, and walked the same path that she walks, and carried the same loads of swaying greenery. There weren't yachts or halter tops or platform shoes in Göcek then, but I imagine the villagers still shared gossip and complaints, and made plans and dreamed dreams.

A few days in the Dodecanese

October 14

The sign outside the ferry office door advised, "Bodrum to Kos everyday 9 a.m." The man in the ticket office said, "9 o'clock, but be here at 8:30," and 9 a.m. was clearly printed on our tickets. But when we arrived at 8:20 a.m. we were told to "hurry please, to passport control" where, waiting in line behind a confused gaggle of girls from Britain, our passports were taken from us and we were rushed aboard a fully loaded boat. We stood on the ferry's tail, temporarily stateless. A man, running, reached across the watery gap with our passports, and the ferry chugged away from the dock. It was 8:37 a.m.[3]

We had arrived in Bodrum the day before, hopping from town to town on three different midibuses in a journey that took nearly five hours. This was our first visit to Bodrum since our arrival in Turkey three months ago. Then we had little time to look around. Now we see that Bodrum has changed a lot in the three short years since our last visit. The main pedestrian street is newly paved and there are new sidewalks and new palm trees; but the town is still filled with ill-clad holiday-makers on cheap package tours, tacky tourist shops, and booming discos. Only the Bodrum dogs, the castle, and a few long-time shops remind us of the village we first saw and enjoyed nearly ten years ago. Tourism has brought gold into town, but it's in the process of destroying the goose.

Kos Town, capitol of the Greek island of Kos in the Dodecanese, is also touristy, but it has the advantage of being a larger town with a longer history of tourism and is, therefore, more settled, less hectic, and less overbuilt. Greek and Roman ruins sprout unexpectedly all through the little city, and spacious parks still bloom with bougain-villea and red hibiscus. We arrived about 9:30 a.m. and took the first room offered us by a woman who met the ferry. It was a small room without amenities, but it was in the heart of the old town, and had direct access to a rooftop patio. We were satisfied. This trip is a required one: our Turkish visas are only good for three-month stays and so we must leave the country and re-enter with a new visa. Trav-eling to Greek islands is a commonplace for the foreigners who make Turkey their home. And for foreign residents living in nearby Greece, a trip to Turkey is likewise a common event.

It doesn't take long for even the dullest tourist to ascertain that Kos was the home island of Hippocrates. Tee-shirts emblazoned with the Hippocratic oath, in every language and color, flap in shop-aw-ning breezes. The ruins of the 4th century B.C. Asklepium, or hos-pital, are just outside the city. Downtown near the castle is a large plane tree, its branches propped up with steel poles and surrounded by protective fencing. This is said to be the very tree Hippocrates stood under as he taught. We agreed it looked old, but were not con-vinced it had lived more than 2,300 years.

The island itself is long and narrow and flat, except for a rugged spine of mountains running down one side of its length. There are a number of small villages on the island, in addition to the city of Kos, and the island's population, according to a brochure, is 21,334. A 14th-century Crusader castle echoes the one in Bodrum a few miles across the sea and occupies one arm of the town's small harbor. Its long, high stone walls offer a smooth face to the Aegean, with few of those turrets or crenelations that make castles so picturesque. Inside though, it's a different story, for the walls hide a deep moat and inner fortress. Both of us love castles, so we spent most of the morning wandering around the ramparts and investigating hidden tunnels and stairwells.

In the evening we walked through the ruins of the Roman baths. Here was a well-preserved mosaic floor, and one almost-complete marble tub for two, with three pristine white steps still leading from each side into the deep basin. The remains of red tile plumbing could clearly be seen all around us. From the baths we climbed up to a small plaza, past a Byzantine ruin, and had ouzo in an outdoor cafe before moving on to dinner in the square.

After spending three uninterrupted months in Turkey, we found ourselves awed by the sophistication of Kos. So many goods in the stores, such a look of orderliness, so many cars. We spent most of the following day wandering around ooh-ing and ahh-ing over the moderness of Greece.

The next morning we caught an 8 a.m. excursion boat to Nissiros for another two-night stay. Nissiros is a small island with a volcano at its heart. There are only four villages here, housing a total of about 1,000 people. Our hotel, a nice three-star affair that closed for the season the day we left, sat on a hillside overlooking Mandraki, the largest town and only port. There is no natural source of water on this island; it is shipped in from neighboring Kos. The hotels, therefore, extend their supply by adding sea water to the tap water. Since we usually drink bottled water when traveling the only noticeable effect was to our hair, which stiffened and ballooned to abnormal proportions.

Mandraki is not one of those picturesque villages you see on postcards. Not every building is sparkling white, and not every door is blue. Nevertheless, it is charming. It sits on a hillside under a tall

cliff crowned by a monastery and a castle ruin. Its tiny beach is littered with brightly-painted fishing boats, and the four or five tourist
shops are scattered along the winding, arms-width-wide streets. It's
an easy place to get lost in, and in fact we did. The weather cooled
while we were there, but not enough to keep us from the outdoor
cafes. We had our before-dinner ouzo beside the sea, and dinner in
the town square higher up the mountain.

On our second day on Nissiros, early in the morning, we rented
a motor scooter and went up to the volcano, 17 kilometers away and
2,100 feet high. This is Polyvotis, named for the fiery titan who "so
incurred Poseidon's wrath that the sea god ripped off a piece of Kos
with his trident and hurled it on top of Polyvotis as he attempted
to swim away. This became the island of Nissiros and the miserable
Polyvotis, pinned underneath, eternally sighs and fumes through the
volcano which took his name."

For someone who suffers from a fear of heights, the volcano
road was terrifying. It wound upward through hairpin curves with
the sea sickeningly far below. When we topped the caldera we lost
the sea view but won a steep descent down into the massive crater,
through yet more hairpin turns. The inside of the volcano, about four
kilometers in diameter, is no longer cultivated, but as we traveled the
twisting road downward we were surrounded by narrow terraces
separated by crumbling rock walls and old, bent olive trees. Here and
there we saw the remains of stone houses, but the residents left long
ago, and the worker in the lone cafe overlooking the oozing mud of
the inner, still active crater had the vast sunken valley to himself.

We parked our sleek yellow scooter and hiked the 100 meters
down into the smaller crater, where sulfur fumes, hissing steam, and
bubbling mud are the only signs of life. We and one other couple

were the only tourists at this hour, though later in the morning bus-loads of daily excursionists would make a brief stop.

The Greeks love to put small churches in inaccessible places. I don't know what belief, or personality quirk, inspires these sitings but their stark-white outlines against a cobalt sea or sky make them compelling to the traveler. From the depths of the mud-caked crater we could see one of those blue-roofed buildings high on the outer crater rim, so we climbed out and boarded the scooter and started up a rutted dirt road. The church at the top is a tiny one, but its location on this narrowest bit of rim means there's a view of the crater on one side and the sea on the other. Not surprisingly, and despite the terrible road, there were hints of a closed restaurant adjoining the church. On this day, however, there was no sign of life and the wind whipped around us with unpleasant speed. We left Polyvotis to his eternal sighs and went to the village of Nikia for lunch.

Nikia is even more charming than Mandraki. It sits high on the steep slope of the island and its streets, fit only for donkeys or motorbikes, wrap themselves around the whitewashed cube houses and lead into a tiny enclosed square. Here the inevitable bougainvil-lea blooms, and a blue-doored cafe serves light lunches and drinks. There are no tourist shops, and we shared the village with just a few other foreigners: three Americans and a Greek-Swiss family from our hotel. We wandered until we found a second cafe overlooking the sea and the island of Tilos. The tables in the shade of a large tree proved irresistible, and we settled down to a leisurely lunch before heading off on the scooter for more exploring.

Several hours later we were back in Mandraki, deciding that we had better find out about the ferry to Rhodes. This proved difficult, as the Greeks have the civilized notion of closing everything in the afternoon, from 1:30 or so, until around 5 or 6 p.m. Faced with this dilemma we did the only thing possible: we went to the hotel and took a nap. In the evening we ventured out again, asking several travel agents and shop owners where the ferry office was, or what they could tell us about the schedule. Anyone living on a small island, we assumed, would surely know the ferry schedule by heart. Well. Turns out no one knows for sure, but they think it leaves at 7 a.m., or maybe 7:30, or possibly 8 a.m., and they think you can buy tickets on board, but there's a woman who sets up a table outside someplace down on the wharf in the morning and you can buy from her, or maybe you can find the office which is somewhere up this street. . . .

Persistence pays, though. We did find the ferry office, closed, so we had our evening ouzo by the sea and went back and it was open. We learned that the ferry would depart at 7:30 a.m., but maybe later, depending on how things go, sometimes it's delayed, it must come from Piraeus, and yes, here was our ticket, paid, in our grasp at last.

Determined to not miss the boat we rose before sunrise the following morning and left the hotel shortly before 7 a.m., as the sky began to lighten. The village was still quiet and the clatter of the wheels on our small suitcase echoed down the cobbled streets. On the wharf we found ourselves alone except for the driver of the island bus, warming his engine. We took seats at a cafe table and waited. By 7:30 other passengers had arrived, the shipping agent had indeed opened her ticket book on a cafe table, and the sun was hinting that it would, eventually, rise over the rim of Polyvotis. Around 8:30 we spotted the big white ferry boat on the horizon, and shortly after 9 a.m. we left Nissiros for Rhodes.

It was a perfect day. The water was glass smooth, the sun uninhibited, the wind nonexistent, and the ferry uncrowded. We rubbed on sunscreen and pulled our white plastic chairs onto the stern deck. As in almost every part of the Aegean, land is always in sight, and we could clearly see the islands of Kos, Nissiros, and Tilos, and the distant shore of Turkey. These islands are primarily desert where, before tourism, income was earned by fishing, sponge diving, and olive growing.

The ferry made a brief stop at Tilos, which has only two small villages but boasts seven castle ruins and a monastery. The entire population is about 500 people so if you're looking for quiet this is the place. Our view from the deck showed a pleasant little town with several cafes, pensions and hotels, and our guidebook says there's a good beach nearby.

The next stop was Simi, with a tiny, almost square harbor surrounded by an Italian hill town. Italy occupied Simi between 1912 and 1945, and left its architecture behind as a reminder. There are high peaks that drop precipitously into the sea. Several islets lay just outside the harbor, making it feel cozily protected and intimate. We decide we will definitely return. The economy here, unfortunately, is driven by tourism, and excursion boats from Rhodes arrive throughout the day during the summer, since it's a quick hour-and-a-half trip (30 minutes by hydrofoil).

Pulling into the Rhodes harbor you practically bump into the most obvious remnant of the island's long pedigree: the medieval, walled city built by the Knights of St. John at the end of that most useless debacle, the Crusades. They had fled from Palestine to Cyprus, and thence to Rhodes, where they stayed 213 years. After a six-month siege in 1522 they surrendered to Suleiman the Magnificent and escaped to Malta. About 6,000 people still live and work within the old city walls, and shops sell everything from designer gold and leather to pornographic coasters and cheap plastic goddesses. Fortunately, the shops line only a few streets. We walked through the huge gates at dusk, determined to find a non-touristy restaurant and see something besides stores. Clouds had filled the sky and rain was probable. It was still pleasant though, so we struck out into the cobbled back lanes.

Truly, this is medieval. The narrow streets twist in haphazard ways, the old buildings lean and tilt at odd angles, the stone is golden and brown and warm to the touch. It is much bigger than we expected. Some alleys are crossed by stone arches, wide or narrow. Everywhere there are discoveries: a bizarre piece of carved marble high in a stone wall; a hidden, blooming courtyard; a glorious pink bougainvillea framing a grayed wooden door. We succumbed to a first-class art gallery and by the time we dragged ourselves away it was dark, and distant lightning and thunder provided a theatrical backdrop to our wanderings. Few people were about. Verily, Sean Connery in monk's robes might step round the next corner demanding that we hie ourselves back to the Scriptorium. The old gas lights, now electrified, were glimmering along the alleys, and we drifted left and right, not knowing or caring where. Occasionally we passed restaurants or small pensions, but nothing appealed. Then we found a tiny hole-in-the-wall cafe and stepped inside.

It was brightly lit, with three tables and a counter dividing the kitchen from the customers. A couple, eating, occupied the table nearest the door. A man, woman, and child looked at home at the second, and a child's toys littered the third. We hesitated, but the woman quickly rose and cleared the toys, insisting we sit down. She offered the basic Greek tourist menu or the food cooking on the stove so we chose the latter—a dish of stewed vegetables—and settled in.

This was like eating in someone's kitchen; in fact, we probably were. The woman in charge identified herself as the child's grand-mother. Grandpa sat at the family table, minding the boy—a four- or five-year-old who was the center of everyone's attention. But grand-pa was tired and kept dozing off. Pretty soon the daughter came in and prepared dinner for the child. Then a friend dropped by and there was much loud, animated discussion. (The Greeks are great at this. Sometimes you think they're going to haul off and slug one another, but instead they kiss and walk away perfectly happy.) Our food arrived and was delicious. Throughout our stay the thunder grew louder and the lightning flashes more dramatic, and when we finally stepped back into the stone alley we agreed that the weather, the dinner, and the setting were perfectly matched, and we couldn't have asked for a better evening in Rhodes.

The clouds next day decided us against exploring the island so we went back to the old town and it rained.

"This is unusual," said the shop owners.

"We never have rain in October," they said.

"One year we had NO rain all year!" said one.

Well, it didn't just rain, it opened up and poured buckets.

When the water rose to a depth of one-to-two inches we thought maybe we should buy an umbrella. We stopped in a small clothing shop, picked one out, paid for it, and returned to the door. The water in the street was now ankle deep and getting deeper. It poured out of the medieval gargoyles in great arching torrents. It raced down the hilly streets, rippling over the rough cobblestones like any moun-tain brook. It ran clear, then muddy, then clear. Merchants rushed to bring merchandise inside, and trapped tourists gazed longingly out doorways. We spent 40 minutes watching all this with two friendly saleswomen; then the sun came out, the water ran off into the harbor, the shopkeepers restored their displays, and the tourists went back to shopping. We found the inevitable cafe in the inevitable tree-filled square, and had lunch.

The next morning we took the hydrofoil from Rhodes to Marmaris, Turkey, a 55-minute trip that was only a half-hour late departing. We breezed through customs with new three-month visas, walked a few blocks to the otogar, and after a two-hour bus ride we were back in our apartment by 1 p.m. The sun was shining, the sky was clear, and we figured we had each gained about five pounds. A pretty good adventure.

A midi-bus

Inflation 101

Ray writes: October 23

Today we purchased a ream of paper at the stationery store in Göcek. The five-hundred-sheet ream cost TL500,000 ($5.61). If we had purchased this ream back in 1987 and paid for it with the same number of Lira it would have cost us $62.50. Then the dollar bought TL800; today it buys TL89,000. We watch the rate change every other day or so, when we walk by Zeki's news stand. Before we leave Turkey, we'll see the dollar go higher than TL100,000. Inflation has devastating effects on municipal workers, teachers, pensioners and the like. This year the Turkish Central Bank plans to "brake inflation" at 80 percent.

Nurhan, the owner of the stationery store, and her husband and another couple were seated at a table behind the counter enjoying a nice breakfast when we went in. We accepted her offer of a glass of tea, which we sipped while we shopped. She works up to fifteen hours a day in the store while fitting in the care of two children and a house. Her husband works at a nearby building materials shop. Few people here know the phrase "leisure time." I wonder what they think of us, being here for a year and not working.

Turkish tech

October 28

We've been awash in technology this week. It started Sunday when Huseyin's TV satellite dish arrived. These small dishes—about 24 inches in diameter—are popular in Turkey as you need only the purchase price to get one going. There are no translators or other devices required, nor additional monthly fees. You pay your $250 or so for the dish, aim it at the satellite, and plug it in. Then you can watch all the *futbol* you want.

Two snappily-dressed young technicians delivered the dish, and we watched the installation from our living room window. They first tried Huseyin's back deck but reception was "problem," so the dish and its umbilicaled TV were lugged from spot to spot across the field. All this activity drew Mehmet and Ipek, and a fellow from across the hall, and they all offered advice and watched the picture fade in and fade out as the TV jogged across the now-desolate garden. Finally Huseyin was satisfied, and the dish came to rest 30 feet from the house in the middle of grandma's field. There it was nailed to a tree stump that was then buried in the dirt. Later in the day the connecting wire, a thick white one, was stretched from the dish up to a branch in the nearest eucalyptus, then over a shrub-like tree and into his apartment. No one but us seems to have noticed that part of it droops lower than cow-horn height.

Our next brush with technology came when we decided to purchase a gas heating stove. Like all apartments here ours has a hole in the wall for a stove-pipe connection, but our landlords had not installed one, choosing instead to use electric heaters. Electricity is expensive in Turkey, however, so it was only a matter of time before we succumbed to the lure of warm, cheap *gaz*. Luckily our occasional neighbors, Helen and Bob, also wanted a stove and knew that Mr. Dim sold them, so a trip to Dim's supermarket was obviously in order.

The Dim Market is our nearest grocery as well as a source of *gaz* canisters for the cooking stove, and wood for the fireplace. Mr. Dim is only about 50, but he has a long white droopy fu-manchu mustache. He's not unfriendly but he's usually too preoccupied to smile, and he can always be found seated at the big carved wooden desk in the center of his shop, an executive at the heart of his empire. His cash register is a cardboard box (just lean back and dip your hand in and grab those lira notes) and his receipts are penciled tallies scratched on torn pieces of cigarette cartons. Dim seldom leaves his chair because his minions (son Ramazan, various unidentified workers, and occasionally Mrs. Dim) are there to fetch and carry for him. Everyone in town knows Dim and everyone drops in occasionally to chat or have tea and, usually, to make a purchase.

Mr. Dim's empire, which he shares with at least one brother, consists of two Dim markets, a *pansiyon*, the local *ekmek fabrikasi* (bread factory) and several other varied and discriminating enterprises. One of these enterprises sells stoves. Our purchase of said item involved several trips to Dim's and several conversations with Ramazan. It entailed climbing into R's van and driving three blocks (like Californians, Turks think if you've got a car, by Allah you should drive it) to his uncle's shop above Dim Market #2, to view a room full of dusty, lonely stoves. At last, after a two-day wait, it involved delivery and installation, and several trips back and forth for various lengths of stovepipe and other missing pieces.

Our stove, now standing in a corner of the living room, is a dull, dark brown cylinder of pipe with a gas burner in the bottom and a gas hose out the back, leading to a gas bottle a few meters away. Helen says it looks ethnic. This is her polite English way of not noticing the dent in the side and the oxidized finish. We love our stove though. Its flat round top is the perfect size for holding the teakettle or roasting chestnuts, and it adds a warm glow to our cooling evenings. Sometimes it's hard to beat basic Turkish technology, especially when it costs only $20, plus *gaz*.

Between the time we ordered our stove and the time it was delivered we went with Bob and Helen on their sailboat to Marmaris. They went to get an estimate on new teak decking and we went along for the ride. It's about 50 miles by sea, along an unspoiled, rugged mountain coastline, and into one of the world's prettiest harbors. We left Göcek at 8:30 a.m., turned on the auto pilot, and motor-sailed away under sunny skies, arriving shortly after 4 p.m. Marmaris is a different place without tourists and we enjoyed poking around in "real" stores. We hired a taxi and went to Migros, a large supermarket with unheard of delicacies (canned peanuts!). Loaded with goodies we returned to the boat for dinner aboard, and went to sleep to the sound of honking horns and tooting boat whistles—Turkey had won a *futbol* game.

We left Marmaris at noon the following day under cloudy skies. A few miles out the wind steadied and the sails went up and stayed up for most of the day. The sun set about six and within a half-hour we were enveloped in darkness; a pale moon behind clouds and sparks of phosphorescence in our wake were the only light. The coastal mountains, previously friendly, loomed large, dark, and ominous. But this was a well-equipped, 48-foot yacht, and technology eased

our path. The radar screen looked miles into the distance and the satellite navigation system hummed and beeped and flashed little red
lights in four directions. Our course took us east up the coast, around
a headland and then north, threading through some of Fethiye Bay's
12 islands. Ray had the helm, monitoring speed, distance, and direction and regularly peering through a hand-held, specially-lighted
compass, taking readings on the lighthouses we passed. Bob and
Helen sat below monitoring equipment, following the boat's progress on the chart, and signaling course changes. My job was to relay
compass readings and way-point distances between helm and chart
table. I did it extremely well.

After nearly three hours of this we motored safely through the
last island channel and pulled into Göcek's nearly empty harbor.
The Zuhal bar, on the harbor front, was having its final night of the
season, a drink-the-bar-dry party, but we were too tired to go. Technology, we decided, can be exhausting, and Göcek's quiet streets and
tin-pipe stoves looked mighty good.

Marmaris harbor

Simplicity lives here

Ray writes: November 3

When packing for our Turkey trip, I threw in an old book of applied technology projects—solar ovens, distillers, water heaters and the like. I thought it would be great fun to assemble some of them from the scrap material I would find during our stay.

It wasn't long before I discovered that scrap anything virtually doesn't exist here. I've seen no scrap heaps, used clothing stores, second-hand stores, or auto-wrecking yards (I'm convinced that if a small group of Turks were turned loose in an average American auto wrecking yard, half the cars would be driven out within 24 hours). Clothing is passed down, lumber is reused, appliances are fixed, things that long ago would have been in an American landfill are kept going and going and going. Because so many things are expensive or difficult to find, Turks are by necessity improvisational, and sometimes comic, geniuses.

Rick tells a wonderful story about observing two Turks at a building site near his home. They had two pieces of hose; neither was long enough to span the needed distance, nor did they have a hose coupler. When one worker found a wheelbarrow with a pipe frame he took the end of one hose and slipped it into one of the handles. The second hose was fastened to the other handle the same way, and when the water was turned on it flowed right through the wheelbarrow. Voila! Yet I can easily imagine myself driving five miles (each way) to the nearest Home Depot to purchase the needed part. Bravo to simplicity.

Blue water, deep bay

November 5

It is election day in America. The months-long, clamorous presidential campaign has been only a whisper here, heard infrequently and filtered through the staid voices of the BBC or the earnestly-trying-to-be-objective VOA. We have not missed it. The debates, the ads, and the endless wrangling passed us by this year, leaving us to make our choices unswayed by cant. Turkish mail being what it is, we made those choices and mailed our ballots weeks ago, and promptly lost interest.

With that patriotic duty satisfied it was no hardship to say yes when invited by our neighbors to spend election day sailing, with a lunch at Deep Bay. We hadn't seen Deep Bay, though we had heard about it. It's a favorite spot for local yachties, and the restaurant there is owned by the family who own our apartment building. Yuksel, the oldest son, runs the restaurant and lives there during the tourist season.

The sun is warm as we leave the dock shortly after 8 a.m., heading south across a glass-smooth sea. And the air is perfectly still when, 30 minutes later, we motor slowly into Laundry Bay, named for its freshwater spring. There we join eight other sailboats quietly floating over their shallow-water shadows. The anchor clanks noisily down, and 20 minutes later the aroma of frying bacon entices the five of us—Bob, Helen, her sister Pat, Ray and I—into the sunny cockpit for a breakfast of orange juice, coffee, scrambled eggs, grilled tomatoes, and of course bacon, bread, butter, and local honey. Not a shabby start to the day.

After a short swim by the heartier members of our party we continue the journey south. There's still only a slight, wafting breeze, but the sound of the engine is disturbing the peace of our morning so the sails go up and we spend a quiet 90 minutes drifting across smooth water at about two knots. No need to hurry. I stretch out on the stern deck and watch the ripples of our wake spread over the surface of the water and meld again with the flat, deep sea.

Eventually Bob gives a few warning toots on the boat's horn to alert Yuksel, who is expecting us, of our imminent arrival. Then we turn right and motor though a narrow gap into the bay. You will not be surprised to learn that it is beautiful. Surrounded by steep, pine-covered bluffs that drop straight into the sea, the cove is, as one would expect from its name, deep and blue. A sharp left turn inside the entrance takes us into a smaller V-shaped inlet, and there at the bottom of the V is a beach and Yuksel's restaurant.

It looks at first as though no one is stirring, then smoke is spotted rising from the fire, and a figure ambles toward the kitchen. We tie up to the jerry-built wooden dock and traipse ashore to say hello. And as you'd expect—this is Turkey after all—despite being the only diners on this last day of seasonal operation, we are each given a hearty welcome, including the traditional handshake and a kiss on both cheeks.

Tradition satisfied, we find there will be a slight delay. The wood fires must blaze higher, a table must be set, the food prepared. So after ordering (three chicken, one fish, one lamb shish), we head back to the boat for a swim. There is no wind in the cove and the sun beats down from a cloudless sky. But despite the warm air the water has cooled considerably in recent weeks and while I'm flailing around trying to overcome the shock I miss seeing a giant green sea tortoise about 30 feet away. The tortoises are a tourist attraction along this part of the coast, because they return here annually to lay their eggs. This one, disgusted with having an audience perhaps, quickly dives, and though we coaxingly call after it, never reappears.

After swimming and a change of clothes it's back to the cockpit for an aperitif—and Helen really does say, "Pimms anyone?"—and then we all trundle across the ramshackle wooden pier to our waiting table standing alone in the sunshine. Its bright red cloth, sparkling wineglasses, flowers, and waiting hors d'oeuvres would be enough to make it inviting, but the peppers and eggplant in grandma's homemade, garlicky yogurt clinch it.

This restaurant's setting is idyllic, well protected from southern breezes, with plenty of shade from summer's heat. From the rocky beach in front of us the water stretches away to the mountains on the opposite side, giving the illusion that we're sitting beside a small mountain lake. Behind our table a crescent-shaped rock wall forms a bar, with tree stumps for stools. At the bottom of the V, back against the bluff, is the kitchen—a small stone building with a red-tiled roof. Between the two are three fire pits where Yuksel rules with the help of two young assistants.

A long grape arbor, its twining leaves thin and yellow now, parallels the beach to our right. Piled under it are enough wooden tables and chairs to seat 60, ready for a dull winter. A tiny, weathered wooden shack on stilts, in the shallows on the far side of the cove, is Yuksel's summer residence, his home eight months a year. His transportation, a peeling blue and white wooden fishing boat, is tied nearby.

This restaurant is typical of its kind, but its eleven years of operation have given it an established air that many beach-side places lack. Two years ago the local *jandarma* made a tour of beach restaurants, destroying all they could in order to limit competition for the in-town, tax-paying establishments. They do this every few years. Here, we're told, they knocked down all but the stone kitchen. But the banana trees and fruit trees and flowering shrubs weren't harmed, and they and the new-old rock walls and structures suggest serene permanence, disguising what is essentially a transient existence.

It is mid-afternoon now and we are still eating, munching through a second order of Yuksel's famous French fries. The food, cooked over wood fires, has been superb; the wine exceptionally drinkable. Life is good, as it should be after such a meal, and we are content. Behind us the sun is sinking, its light now partially screened by the pines that top the hills; its heat waning in the afternoon breeze. Reluctantly we order our Turkish coffees and prepare to say goodbye. Yuksel joins us at the table and at Helen's request "reads" her coffee grounds.

"This, see here," pointing to a drip outside the cup, "was problem; but now, no problem."

Looking into Pat's cup he says, "Too much work. But better soon, no problem."

Thinking those are pretty good fortunes, the rest of us decide not to press our luck, and prepare to say goodbye. But before leaving we have three large and several small fresh fish pressed on us because, "No more customers, no restaurant, tomorrow finish." Then, after effusive farewells, we settle into an easy 90-minute sail back to Göcek, arriving home to news of the president's reelection.

To Cappadocia

November 15

We rented a car and drove to Cappadocia last week; 2,000 kilometers across a dramatically varied landscape, with so much to see and be surprised at that we came home suffering from severe cases of visual over-stimulation.

Cappadocia lies 160 miles southeast of Ankara on Turkey's high central plain. Three large volcanoes mark the eastern and southern edges of the region and from them, millennia ago, spewed "tuff," a pumice-like material that covered the area then gradually eroded to create what must be one of Earth's eeriest landscapes. You have probably seen pictures of Cappadocia. I hope so, because it's almost impossible to adequately describe. It's as though some child goddess spent a day making oddly-shaped mud pies and left them to bake in the sun. Then trolls and troglodytes carved them out for homes. Perhaps the child was Aphrodite because the rocks that the Turkish Tourist Authority modestly calls "fairy chimneys" looked to us more phallic than fairyic.

Our first stop was Antalya, the fastest growing city in Turkey. Located on the Mediterranean coast, Antalya is a favorite destination for Germans, Russians, and yachties. The nearby beaches are lined with multi-story hotels but at the city's heart sits a small "old town" surrounding the tiny, original harbor. Finding our way through the winding hillside streets was confusing, but the friendly *pansiyon* made it worth the struggle. Old wooden Ottoman buildings—some nothing but ramshackle shells—line the twisting streets. Here at least tourism has been a blessing, for these decrepit shells, with their over-hanging, latticed balconies, are being given new life as renovated *pansiyons*, small hotels, restaurants, and the inevitable tourist shops.

From Antalya we drove north through the rugged Taurus Mountains that edge the Anatolian plateau, then east across endless fields of wheat stubble, past tiny, desolate, mud-hut villages and grand 700-year-old Seljuk caravansaries to Nevşehir, where we could see the snow-covered, 12,700 foot peak of Erciyes Dag rising directly ahead of us. Finally, shortly after dark, we drove down a steeply curving hill into the village of Göreme.

We awoke next morning in an arched vault—a small, bare stone room with two shelf-like niches carved deep into opposite walls and two paned windows looking out through leafless branches onto a visual cacophony of rock. Outlined against a clear sky were fawn-colored tuff cones honeycombed with rooms and passages scarred with the deep-shadowed openings that are doors and windows and pigeon roosts. A jumble of small square and rectangular buildings grew randomly on the cones like sharp-edged carbuncles and all—linked by narrow dirt trails—was piled higgledy-piggledy in front of us, filling the windows from bottom to top. We walked out into this madness to the *pansyion* dining room and had our breakfast in a cave; a warm, pleasant room with red-checked table cloths. Mozart accompanied our munching through the standard Turkish serving of boiled egg, sliced tomatoes, cucumbers, white cheese, olives, and of course bread, butter, and jam.

There is a great deal to see in Cappadocia. People have been carving out homes and lives here since at least Neolithic times, and those who called these rocks home include the Hatti, Hittites, Persians, and Greeks. The Romans annexed it in 66 B.C. After the

Romans came the Byzantines, the Seljuks, the Ottomans, and finally, in 1923, the Turkish Republic. A third of the Göreme population still lives in rock-hewn caves. They still drive gaily painted horse-drawn wagons, still plant tiny vineyards and plow small fields, and still gather pigeon dung for use as fertilizer.

Göreme was the center of a large Christian population during the Roman and Byzantine periods, and they carved hundreds of chapels and churches into the soft rocks; some say one for each day of the year. The open-air museum containing some of these was our first stop. We took pity on a guide who looked ill and followed him from church to church as he pointed out the saints and stories depicted on the frescoed walls. Most of the paintings have been defaced or obliterated, for Moslems believe that depicting any man or beast is an affront to God. After an hour spent being impressed by the ingenuity of the builders and depressed by the stupidity of man we climbed into the car and drove to Ürgüp, another tuff-built town, and had lunch.

We are objects of curiosity, despite the annual influx of thousands. Maybe it's the season; there aren't many tourists in November. The local Turks are less friendly and far more conservative than the coastal residents we're used to. There is obvious poverty too, and for the first time we are the focus of animosity when, leaving a picturesque and famous stone church, very young boys throw rocks at our car. This was shocking in its rarity and shook our complacency, but it was a reminder of the undercurrents of poverty and unhappiness that exist in Turkey, a country we sometimes view through admittedly rosy glasses.

From Ürgüp we passed through the valley of fairy chimneys and finally, late in the afternoon, drove into Zelve, a site occupied as recently as 1953. The honeycombed cliffs of its three adjoining valleys had weakened dangerously so the population was moved into New Zelve and their way of life effectively lost. The valley walls are pockmarked with churches, mills, monasteries, a small mosque, and many, many dwellings, some with decoratively carved doors and windows. We had barely begun our exploration—with the help of a young, machine-gun toting *jandarma* who showed us the way up a rock face—when the sun dropped behind the cliffs and the air quickly chilled. We bought a glass of tea for our helpful policeman and decided to return the following morning.

I won't bore you with endless descriptions of rock caves which, though remarkable, all began to look alike. We passed up the underground cities, reportedly as many as seven stories deep where communities and their livestock lived in protected isolation for years on end, and chose instead to drive to the Ilhara Valley, a small gorge at the southern edge of Cappadocia.

Here the Melendiz river has cut deeply into the soft volcanic tuff, and green trees and tall grasses are watered by the burbling stream. The shaded riverbed lies in sharp contrast to the pale rock and barren land surrounding the canyon, and the prospect is pleasant and lush in comparison. The starkness of the northern, rock-hewn landscape is missing here, and the sound of water splashing on rock is a welcome change. A few small villages hug the banks between stream and canyon walls, and many old, frescoed churches—some dating from the 4th century—are carved deep into the soft stone.

Near a village we pass three teenage girls traditionally dressed in bright patterns. Ray can't resist a photo so he parks and climbs out of the car to ask their permission. Turkish men are usually quite willing to be photographed, but the women often refuse. Whether this is due to shyness or religious scruples or superstition, I can't say. Fortunately, these girls are willing; shy and smiling and nervous and pleased all at once. I watch while he jokes with them and snaps photos, and then they carefully print their addresses in his notebook so he can send them copies. Leaving, he edges the car slowly around them and as I turn to wave goodbye all three girls gracefully blow a kiss in our direction.

Erciyes Dag rises above Cappadocia.

The joy of email

Ray writes: November 20

Lulled into complacency by weeks of sending and receiving email with no problems, we had almost forgotten we were living in a developing country. It wasn't to last. The first sign of trouble came when our Istanbul server dropped from 14,400 bps to 9,600 bps. Sending and receiving was slower but things were working okay. We had more time to sip our tea as we watched our messages zoom off into cyberspace. Around the first of November it became impossible to send an email to anyone from Göcek at any speed. Email *yok* (finished). Despite scores of tries, everything failed. It was reminiscent of the forty or so tries necessary to get a call through back in 1987. Attempts to reach our U.S. server's customer service by telephone were not successful, the last call resulting in me waiting on hold for 20 minutes (not inexpensive from Turkey) listening to a recording stating that a customer service representative would be with me "shortly." Sounds like things are normal in America.

Sunday passed, then Monday, and still no connection. Tuesday evening I tried the Ankara number, two numbers in Istanbul, one in Izmir, all with no success. I then tried to make a connection through Nice, Paris, and London, all with the same result. As a last resort I dialed the number we have for access in Eugene, Oregon and was able to send our report. The things we do for love.

On the road

November 25

The people you meet and the sights flying past the car window
are as much a part of any road trip as your destination. In a country
like Turkey this is even more evident; sameness and routine will only
be found in the car's interior.

The landscape itself changes rapidly, for Turkey's terrain, as our
Country Study tells us, "is structurally complex. A central massif com-
posed of uplifted blocks and downfolded troughs, covered by recent
deposits and giving the appearance of a plateau with rough terrain,
is wedged between two folded mountain ranges that converge in
the east." Turkey's highest peak, Mount Ararat (about 16,700 feet), is
located in the far east, near the Iranian and Armenian borders.

It is not the landscape, however, but the living culture that
makes driving in this country an experience. As we pull into a large
service station outside Antalya, a man in a dusty white coat immediately offers a tray filled with small plastic cups of tea; he weaves
from car to truck to tractor in the busy station, making sure everyone
has their complimentary drink. In another station we are helped by a
cheerful boy of about 12 who is alone and in charge. He competently
fills our tank and supplies the engine with a liter of oil. All along
the way we see elaborate new *benzine* stations with restaurants,
mini-markets, and huge parking areas. Some of these wear familiar
names, like Mobil and BP.

Since road construction is rampant, these stations increasingly
sit beside smooth new highways. In most cases the new highways

bypass towns and villages, but some follow old footpaths through the "centrum." Despite the widening and the increased traffic, the villagers still consider these roads their personal property, so it's not surprising that we twice came round a bend on a four-lane divided road to find two women in the street shaking dust from a large rug. Nor is it surprising to find motor vehicles or carts coming toward you on the wrong side, because, after all, they're only going a kilometer or two, and besides, there are few passages through the high median divider.

This clash of decades and even centuries is reflected in the traffic we encountered: horse-drawn carts, slow tractors pulling trailers, poky midibuses and big, high-speed long-distance buses; donkeys laden with sticks, motorcycles with up to four people astride, speeding red BMWs, oblivious pedestrians in unexpected places—perhaps even holding a conversation—and various and sundry livestock. In Göreme we waited as four camels paused in the street, after a busy day of posing for tourists, to drink from the village fountain, while behind them a nine-year-old impatiently swatted cows who only wanted to graze on the median-strip flowers. On the highway no signs announce "open range"; it just is. Cows, sheep, goats, donkeys, horses, a running pack of dogs; all or any could be around the next bend. None of these, of course, are wired for lights, which is why we don't drive after dark.

The Anatolian interior is more religiously conservative than the coast, and some of the gray and brown towns appear inhabited only by men wearing the gray and brown clothes they favor, with their colorful knit caps as sole relief from deadly dullness. There is something disconcerting about a town where only men are seen. I think of war zones or prison yards—unhealthy places. The men fill the streets; idling, walking, sitting, standing, staring.

It was outside the towns, on the roads and in the fields, that we saw the women, dressed in their colorful calico pantaloons and white headdresses. Their costumes changed slightly as we got further from the coast. The headdresses became more elaborate, the scarves got longer and hung further down their backs. Pantaloons became fuller and the crotch dropped lower until they were wearing full gathered skirts with holes in the bottom for their feet. Occasionally we saw a scarf pulled across the bridge of a nose, or a woman covered entirely in black, but this was rare. Western dress was seen only in tourist areas or sizable towns.

It is the Turkish women who seem to work hardest, and I watched them guiltily from the comfort of our rented car, bending low to pick cotton, squatting over a plastic tub doing laundry, guiding a horse or donkey with a plow, scattering seed, cutting grapes,

Sheep hog the road.

beating raw wool clean in a stream, herding cows and goats, stooping with loaded backs, overseeing flocks of sheep. Rarely do they waste time or exhibit idle hands. Two girls tending sheep beside the road were typically doing double duty: one knitted as she walked, the other spun wool onto a traditional spindle.

To view roadside life more closely we drove into an isolated village on the flat Anatolian plain, a bleak scattering of adobe mud houses along a single-track dirt road. The village looked almost deserted from the highway, yet within seconds of stopping we're surrounded by excited, yelling children. Four young girls, 13 or 14 years old, have planted themselves at my partially open window and are chattering nonstop, stretching their hennaed hands in through the opening to touch my hair, pointing at their own scarf-covered heads and then at my bare one.

On the other side Ray has opened the car door and is taking out his camera, and four or five small boys are all yelling "address! address!" while a man has forced his head through the open door to examine the car's interior. This is all frightening in a way because it is so sudden and unexpected. It reminds me of stopping in Russian villages in 1977, where no one had ever seen a western car or a live American. People would crowd two or three deep around our VW bus to stare in at us; animals in the proverbial zoo.

I try talking to the girls in my pidgin Turkish, but they have no patience with it, they jabber on, pointing over and over again to their covered heads. To mollify them I put on my baseball cap, but that earns me nothing but blank stares. I have a traditional white scarf in the back somewhere, but after a brief, struggling search, I give up looking. Then, out of the babble I hear, "My name is . . ." pronounced slowly, as though a rote phrase, learned long ago and devoid of meaning, has just been recalled.

"Ah, yes," I say, smiling back through the confusion, "my name is Karen." Then I point to the speaker and slowly say, "your name is . . . ." After several tries I get a name, and I move on to the next girl, relieved to have something concrete to communicate. Ray is digging around for a pen and some paper so the boys on his side of the car can write their address. They must have had some contact with foreigners because they have asked for copies of the pictures he takes. This is something we've run into all over Turkey; nearly everyone will agree to having their photo taken if their "address" is also taken down. Such addresses—carefully printed in block letters—are often unrecognizable, the words having no seeming relation to the village or area.

At last Ray climbs back into the car, carefully shutting the door to avoid grasping hands and fingers. A woman has approached and is angrily shooing the boys away. The curious man now stands disconsolate, while one little boy continues to yell, jumping up and down in manic excitement. I shake hands with each of the girls, who are still staring at me in wonder, and we slowly make our way back to the main road.

A sense of frustration always accompanies encounters like these; frustration at our lack of language and knowledge, and the likelihood of being misunderstood and in turn misunderstanding. A feeling, too, that we have interfered somehow, disobeyed the Prime Directive and introduced alien concepts. There is nothing to be done, however, but continue on, hoping our brief stop will have as little effect on them as it will eventually have on us.

No trip down Turkey's highways is complete without at least one stop at a roadside stand. In the lake region west of Konya—after lunch at the Apex Fast Food Center—we came across several stands selling grapes, pickled grape leaves, and *pekmez* (molasses made from grapes). We had been wanting *pekmez* for our French toast, so of course we stopped. The farmer and his wife immediately moved two chairs into the sun and invited us to sit. We sat. Then we were offered several varieties of good, sweet grapes, so we ate while we sat, and made pidgin conversation. While we absorbed the sun and the fruit the farmer sat with us, relaxed, and the woman worked steadily, squatting on the ground sorting bad grapes from good. (All the village women, of whatever age, squat, sitting on their haunches with their feet flat on the ground. When I try this I fall over backwards.)

Eventually we were full of grapes and had extended our Turkish beyond its fragile limits, so we paid for our *pekmez*, and more grapes, and climbed back into the car. The highway, an empty, two-lane, winding strip of gray asphalt, beckoned. I agree with whoever said it is the journey that counts. Destinations are irrelevant.

Camels delivering firewood.

A Thanksgiving fable

November 28

Once upon a time there was a woman living in a far foreign land who longed for a real Thanksgiving turkey (well, Christmas turkey actually, but this is a fable). Every year she would ask the local butcher if he could find a real turkey for her, and every year the butcher would sigh heavily, and sadly reply "*hayir*."

And every year the woman asked all her friends who were going off to the distant island if they would look for a Thanksgiving turkey, and every year they returned home sad-faced and empty handed. Once, long ago, they had found a turkey. It was wrapped in strange plastic with unfamiliar writing, and it had an even stranger red button in its breast. The woman living in the far foreign land had never seen such a thing, but she cooked it anyway and all her friends and family loved it, and said it was a wonderful thing. But the next year, again, there were no turkeys to be found, not even strange ones.

Then one day, about a month before Thanksgiving, the woman heard a rumor that the butcher would have turkeys for the expat holiday. She rushed down to the shop, burst in, and gasped, "Is it true? Are you really going to sell real turkeys for Thanksgiving?"

The butcher puffed out his chest, grinned his biggest grin, and replied,

"Yes! I am now ordering. How many turkeys do you want?"

"Oh, I only need one," she replied. "A small one."

"Only one?" said he.

"Yes, there will just be four of us this year. So I want to order a small turkey, please"

"Very good. You come here two days before your holiday."

Well, you can imagine that the woman in the far foreign land was absolutely ecstatic. A real honest bird for a real honest Thanksgiving. No more trying to stuff chickens or pigeons. No more pretending.

"Why," she thought, "this is almost as good as being at home."

The next few weeks were filled with anticipation and secret preparations, for she wasn't telling her guests; she wanted to surprise them. She would stuff and roast the bird just as she remembered her mother doing, and she would bring it to the table, golden and juicy, ready for carving. Her mouth watered at the prospect. Finally, the day when she would pick up her bird arrived. She gathered her strongest carry-bag, put her lira in her purse, and went to the butcher shop.

"I've come to get my turkey," said she, loving the very words. "Do you have it?"

"Oh yes," replied the butcher happily, "many turkeys I have ordered for your holiday."

"Good!" she replied with great relief, because in far foreign lands one never knows for sure.

The butcher stepped into his back room and brought out a big turkey, plump, white, and glistening.

"It looks wonderful," sighed the woman happily. "But it's so big, and I ordered a small turkey."

"Yes, yes, I know," replied the butcher. And reaching under the counter he brought out a huge cleaver and Whack! he split the bird right down the middle and proudly held it up for inspection.

"Small turkey!" he said with a pleased grin.

But the woman in the far foreign land had fainted.

Moral: Never count your turkeys before they're chopped.

Happy Thanksgiving!

Redefining clean

Ray writes: November 30

It's become necessary for us to redefine some basic words since we arrived in Turkey. One example is the word "clean." Things are now acceptable if they are "almost clean," "fairly clean," or "clean not so long ago."

When Mr. Ozden thoughtfully wrapped my *ekmek* in a sheet of newspaper to keep it clean (the newspaper was three weeks old), or the ice cream vendor pushed ice cream onto the cone with his thumb (he was courteous enough to not use the thumb on his left hand which would have been a serious breach of etiquette), or when the baker selects our cookies with his bare hands, we think "almost clean." No problem.

Once at Dim Market I placed all of my grocery items on the counter (there are no carts or baskets there) while I was having my obligatory cup of *çay* (tea) with Mr. Dim. Mrs. Dim came by and carefully wiped the dust off each item with a rag. This was indeed thoughtful and raised the level of my groceries to "fairly clean." Unfortunately Mrs. Dim isn't always present, so I often find myself rinsing off various bottles, cans and packages when I get home.

When a fly lights on waiting bread, one brushes it away; if an ant or beetle walks across the table, one ignores it and continues to eat. If a utensil drops to the floor in a restaurant, and one is quicker than the cats, it is gracefully returned to the table. These things are thought to be "clean not so long ago."

So as you can see, with our new definition, life has become much simpler. The difference between clean and not-clean has become a comfortable, muddy gray. We have none of those sanitized wrappers to tear off, no plastic gloves to put on, and none of those nasty sterilizing sprays to deal with. This is Turkey.

Bread for sale.

Enough is enough

Ray is sitting across from me reading a book, *Stamboul Train* by Graham Greene. The little brown stove-pipe stove—the one with the ethnic dent and the ionized paint—is heating up a storm, and the carnations in the copper pitcher are going to burst into bloom any minute.

There's a soft glow emanating from the two brass lamps and the little oil lamps on the mantel, and all in all the place feels pretty homey right now. Upstairs I can hear the footsteps of three-year-old Ipek trotting across the floor and occasionally the sound of the water gurgling in the pipes, or a voice calling in the hall. Huseyin, our downstairs neighbor, must be out because I don't hear his TV or any other sounds of activity.

There is a comfortableness to these sights and sounds that I find surprising given that the only items in the room that belong to us are a few books, my walkman, and a photo of our daughter. That one can be content with so few belongings would not surprise most of our neighbors, but it's a condition we're just beginning to appreciate.

December 3

Empty streets, empty sidewalks, and an empty harbor all signify the beginning of winter here in the village. The sun still shines—interrupted only by an occasional rain storm—and the sea still lies glass-smooth most mornings. Afternoon temperatures often hover in the low seventies, but it's just us locals who are here to enjoy it. Back to England, Germany, France, and Holland; back to America, back to Istanbul, to Rhodes, to Tunis or the Red Sea, the tourists and the yachties have flown. The little cobbled street that overflowed with sun-seeking sailors and shoppers now hosts only a handful of pedestrians. The long concrete pier that is Scopea Marina stands empty and naked, like a ragged gray rip in the sea. Even the *gulets* have disappeared, going off to winter moorages for maintenance and repairs. If we didn't know who the locals were before, we surely will soon.

No one seems happier about this than the shopkeepers, who are ready for a break from long hours and demanding customers. The owners declare, almost without exception, that enough money has been earned for the year, "and now it's time to rest and enjoy." We admire this sense of knowing how much money is enough, because it's an idea we struggle with ourselves. Leaving our jobs and coming to Göcek for a year meant evaluating our own "enough" pretty carefully. By most American standards we probably don't have it. Nevertheless, it's good to call a halt occasionally and just enjoy your world. Of course when that world includes a charming village, a gorgeous bay, splendid weather, warm friends and a happy, healthy family, calling a halt is pretty easy to do. We're glad all those tourists don't know what they're missing.

WINTER

Searching for Christmas

December 15

The sun was shining last Sunday and this was a good thing because Sunday is market day. The previous Sunday had been cool and rainy, in fact it had been raining for several days and the field where the market is held was a sea of mud. But this Sunday was warm and sunny and the *pazar* was back to full winter strength and feeling good. I was looking for a zippered sweatshirt like one I had seen a few weeks earlier, and on my second trip through the clothing stalls, I found it. The price was $17.50, but we negotiated and I got my Calvin Klein knockoff for $14.

Every Turkish village or town of any size has at least one weekly *pazar*, and Göcek is no exception. The market is, in many ways, the centerpiece of village life and its weekly occurrence is our chief way of marking time. Everyone goes. It's not only the primary source for veggies and hard goods, it's where you run into friends and exchange the latest gossip. We buy nearly all our veggies at the weekly *pazar*, and sometimes things like Sing-rrr oil and mousetraps. This week there were about 25 vendors selling fruits and vegetables, four selling nuts, two spice vendors, five yardage sellers, 15 hawking clothing, three selling shoes (one featuring Noke [sic] shoes, complete with the swoosh), two kitchenware suppliers, and two tool venders selling harnesses, bells, scythes, rope, axes, and more. You can buy fish straight from a box on the back of a bicycle. You can buy blankets, tablecloths, clothespins, and socks; homemade cheese, olive oil, candy, and cookies; soap, belts, watches, and shampoo; and even a goat or two. And Göcek's market is small.

The nearby towns of Dalaman and Ortaca are more typically Turkish (tourists generally don't go there), and have large *pazars* with five times as many vendors. Most are professionals, moving from market to market and retailing their products. But there are also sellers who come in from nearby villages—whole families arrive on tractors, or motorcycles with sidecars. It's at markets you see the women in village dress, their heads enveloped in elaborately

With the "borek lady" in Ortaca

wrapped turbans, squatting on the ground behind a basket or two. Some have only one kind of product to sell—cauliflower maybe, or apples, or goats, or hand-knit socks. Sometimes we see village men in traditional dress too, dark pantaloons tucked into high boots, heads wrapped. The entire market bustles with shoppers and hums with the sounds of hawkers and bargains being won or lost.

We went to the Ortaca market on Friday with our daughter Jennifer, who arrived here Wednesday morning. She brought news of Oregon flooding, and work, and Christmas preparations, and we were reminded again that we've temporarily escaped all those things. Christmas is almost nonexistent in this Moslem country, and we have not missed it. Knowing, however, that the holiday is usually found in the marketplace, we decided to look hard for it in Ortaca. We found the borek lady, a regular at the Göcek market, who greeted us like long lost family. Jennifer found herself caught in the sticky and effective tendrils of a village jewelry maker and spent $15 extricating herself. Ray found a wool sweater, *"eine kality,"* for $16. But none of us found Christmas. No candles, no wreaths, no gaily wrapped presents, no half-off sales, no repetitive ads, no demands, no hassles, no pressure to please or to prove.

Yesterday, in a sunny garden not far from the Göcek beach, we saw a 20 foot-high poinsettia bush, covered with bright red blossoms. This, and being together, is Christmas enough. The rest we'll gladly forego.

The best laid plans

Ramadan—or Ramazan as the Turks call it—started on Friday, at the first glimpsing of the new crescent moon. This is a time of sunup to sundown fasting and prayer for Moslems, and I've been curious to see how the month-long event will be observed. As infidels we're not expected to participate, but we have been trying to avoid munching on a candy bar or *doner kebab* in public. It was somewhat of a shock then, to see several Turks downing a big lunch yesterday at one of the Çan's outdoor tables.

It's coincidental that the month of Ramazan follows so closely our Christmas and New Year's holidays. Ramazan celebrates the period when the Koran was given to Mohammed and because it's based on a different calendar the month-long period moves forward about 11 days each year. It's followed immediately by the *Fiekerli bayram*, or sugar holiday, when children are given candy or small change by family and friends.

The only holiday we have in common with the Turks is New Year's Eve, and they celebrate that in a big way, with family get-togethers, gifts, and partying. We were in Bodrum this New Year and the streets were crowded with shoppers and high-fashion teenagers anxious to disco the night away. But rumors that gangs from Istanbul were going to circulate through the Bodrum clubs with needles, indiscriminately injecting the HIV virus, kept many away, and it was an unusually quiet night.

None of us were interested in discos—we had to catch a 7 a.m.
bus back to Göcek the next morning—so we spent a cozy evening in
front of Rick and Beverly's fireplace munching Greek paté and sipping Turkish champagne. At midnight we went out on the terrace to
watch random fireworks explode over the floodlit castle.

Christmas was even quieter. Ray and I had to renew our three-
month visas and Jennifer wanted to see Greece, so the three of us
headed for Rhodes and spent Christmas week in Lindos, one of
those picture-postcard villages that are touristic hell in the summer
and next to perfect in deep winter. We spent five nights in two rooms
with kitchenette and balconies overlooking the whitewashed village
(where people have been living for almost 4,000 years), the cobalt
sea, and the castle-topped, jutting cliff that guards two tiny bays.
For most of the week we were the only visitors in town. A Japanese
tour group ghosted through one morning, hiking up to the acropolis
ruins, snapping photos, and boarding the bus for their next stop.

Despite the quiet there was plenty to do, and the few lighted
Christmas decorations scattered through the village were all that was
needed to keep us in a holiday spirit. The weather was clear with a
few drifting clouds, and mornings were spent on the east-facing balcony soaking up the rays of the newly risen sun—a strange sight if
all your life you've seen it go down into the sea, not rise from it. We
walked on the beach collecting rocks and seashells, climbed down
to the tiny harbor where St. Paul landed when he brought Christi-
anity to Rhodes, hiked to the castle and Athenian temple ruins that
dominate the land and seascape, and wove back and forth across the
island in our tiny rented car.

One day we went to Tharri Monastery and met an American
woman, a former Harvard department head who now bears the

official title, "Hermit of the Monastery." She made mountain tea in her little kitchen while we admired the icons she had painted. On Christmas Eve, Ray, Jennifer, and I sat in companionable silence under a grape arbor outside a 1,000 year-old Byzantine church and luxuriated in the quiet darkness, and on Christmas day the two of them played backgammon in a cafe while I sipped retsina and watched the Greeks who gathered to visit, smoke, and gossip.

Our good weather deserted us after the holiday and a storm prevented our ferry crossing from Rhodes to Marmaris. In defiance we took a larger one to Kos where we could more easily cross to Turkey—we thought. But the ferry information was wrong, as usual, and we were stuck in Kos three more nights in three different hotels—all but the last one miserable—straining our pocketbooks and our patience. In the end, however, our delay brought us that unplanned New Year's celebration with good friends and our year ended, as it should have, on a high note.

The flip side of the coin

Ray writes: January 6

Just so you don't think we're on a Club Med or *Travel & Leisure* holiday I thought I would give you an account of some of the hotels and pensions we stay in while traveling, and what we go through to find them. Being on a tight budget and finding suitable accommodations is like walking a tightrope, a compromise between stress, comfort, and affordability. The range of hotels differs considerably and we know there will always be some unexpected surprises. However, two observations can be made: if a hotel has a nice lobby the rooms are usually awful; and Turkish hotels and *pansiyons* are usually cleaner than those in Greece.

On our recent trip to Greece to renew our Turkish visas, we stayed in Marmaris, Turkey the first night, about two and a half hours from Göcek. It's the only way we could catch the early morning ferry to Rhodes. This time of year most of the hotels and *pansiyons* are closed as there are virtually no tourists, just a few hard-core foreigners like us, and the locals.

After a lengthy search through rows of closed high-rise beach hotels, schlepping our luggage of course, we settled for the Otel Kemal, a relatively new and nearly empty seven-story, complete with uniformed staff. The price for two rooms (Jennifer was with us) was $42, with TV and breakfast. After accidentally locking myself out on a fire escape until a puzzled Karen spotted me at dusk, we had dinner in an open-air cafe then turned in for a good night's sleep. Unfortunately, we left the balcony door ajar for ventilation and this became an open invitation to every hungry mosquito in Marmaris. Turkish mosquitoes are small, quiet, quick, and bite hard. At 1:45 a.m., after each of us had donated a generous meal, we turned on all the lights for a battle-to-the-death with our adversaries. In a half-hour we despatched them all, so full and slow were they, and slipped off to sleep until 6:30 a.m.

In Rodos town we walked the short distance from the ferry to the old town in search of a pension. Old town is virtually empty this time of year and the instructions given us by a helpful man led to a pension where one room cost $62. This seemed overpriced for Greece in the winter, and over budget, so we decided to look in the new town where had we stayed last October. Instead of finding open hotels, we found a ghost town reminiscent of San Francisco in *On the Beach*. Empty streets, empty buildings, no people. Patience was running thin by this time, so after walking back to the centrum (with our luggage of course) and still not finding a hotel we hailed the first cab we saw and asked to be taken to any hotel. The cabby drove two long blocks and dropped us off at the Hotel Hermes where, after kissing the driver, we booked a single, spartan room with three beds for $44.50, breakfast included.

The Hermes is centrally located in Rodos, sort-of clean, well aged, with a mostly friendly staff. The bathroom was like most in Turkey and Greece: small, completely tiled, a shower with no curtain (guaranteeing that everything in the room gets thoroughly drenched), and a drain in the center of the floor. This particular bathroom was home to a dead cockroach the size of my thumb, but I evicted him before turning in for another good night's sleep. A radio built into the wall above our pillows didn't work, but the one in the adjacent room did, as we discovered at 5 a.m. when we awoke to the sound of loud Greek folk music. We love Greek folk music, but not at 5 a.m.

Our next stop was the picturesque village of Lindos where we easily found a pension with two new, clean rooms for $41.25, no breakfast. The view from our balcony was absolutely spectacular, and it didn't matter that Karen and I had no hot water in our room or that an army of Greek ants helped us keep our mini-kitchen clean. We walked across the hall to Jennifer's room to shower and cooked in her kitchen. The small can of oil I carry allows me to silence the squeakiest of doors and closets, which I did. We even enjoyed hearing, in the owner's flat below us, the traditional Christmas Eve poker game that went into the wee hours. It was a pleasant and almost restful five nights' stay.

Back in Rodos in preparation for the return ferry to Marmaris the next day, we stayed at the Hermes again, a known quantity. (We knew how large the cockroaches were.) As mentioned above, bad weather kept the once-a-week Rodos/Marmaris ferry from making the trip, so later in the day we took a large ferry north to Kos where, we had been assured, the ferries ran daily to Bodrum.

We arrived in Kos in a heavy downpour at 9:30 p.m. and asked a cabby to take us to a hotel. I thought his choice too expensive so we walked from there toward the harbor and found the Hotel Astron, where for $45 we booked a single room with three beds, including breakfast. Before collapsing in the dingy, over-furnished room, we stuffed the closet with the excess chairs and stools so we could walk without tripping. The marble floors and concrete walls in the hallways amplified every noise and the hollow-core doors were no protection. Throughout the night we heard every footstep and voice in the hallway (and there were, for some reason, lots of them). Each time a door closed it was as if someone had dropped a brick on a table behind us. Bam, bam, bam, all night long. And this is the slow season. Greekologists will tell you that Astron translates as "hell" in English.

The next day we learned that, as usual, we had been given incorrect information, and the ferry to Bodrum runs only three times a week in winter. This did not make us happy. We were facing two more nights in Kos. Greece is about fifty percent more expensive than Turkey and our budget was already stretched. Wearily, we checked out of the hotel from hell, made some exploratory phone calls without success, took a quick look at the nearby Hotel Dismal, wolfed down a Hambo Classic Burger, and found another hotel within walking distance on a seemingly quiet street.

For $24.75 at the Veroniki Hotel we got one room, three beds, and no breakfast. Being somewhat acculturated and even more exhausted, Jennifer and I had managed to look past the shabbiness, the dirt, and the single uncovered light bulb hanging from the ceiling. Karen's reaction was, let's say, different. It was, however, a simple matter to tuck a book under one leg of Jennifer's bed to make it almost level, and to reattach the lamp globe and oil the door hinges. I should be collecting fees for my repair jobs. To avoid the room we went out to a movie—another interesting cultural experience—and returned about 11 p.m. It happened to be a busy Saturday night in Kos and we were to suffer the consequence of Greece's $3.50 per-gallon gasoline—scores of motorcycles and motorbikes, most with straining mufflers that can be heard for blocks. Sleep eluded us until 4 a.m., and at 7 a.m. (Sunday) we were awakened by the sound of drums and trumpets as the Kos military band marched down the street a block away. Did all the Greeks know we had come from Turkey?

With the crew nearing mutiny, suicide, or worse, we staggered across Kos to the Maritina Hotel, the same one (I'm still kicking myself, don't be hard on me) the cabby took us to on our arrival. We quickly checked into two rooms ($54 with breakfast). This time we had lots of clean white towels, a clean floor, clean walls, no ants or cockroaches either dead or alive, a shower curtain (what a concept), TV, mini-bar with grocery store prices, comfortable beds and a friendly staff. We finally did get a good night's sleep before ferrying off to Bodrum the next day to spend New Year's Eve with our American friends and gracious hosts, Rick and Beverly.

In three months we return to Greece to renew our visas.

Kos harbor

Walking ruins

January 13

We rented a car while Jennifer was here and drove east to Antalya to look at some ruins. You would think we would be bored with ruins by now, we've seen so many over the years, but we continue to find them compelling. And every ruin is different. The vastness of Ephesus has nothing in common with the small, lonely temple of Zeus that sits in a dusty green olive grove. The delicate columns of Aphrodisias are nothing like the massive bulk of Didyma.

Sand dunes and cultivated fields dominate the ruins at Patara, a city that was Lycia's principal port, home to an important Apollon oracle, and the 4th century birthplace of St. Nicholas. The harbor is gone now, silted over in the Middle Ages. The site is large, but the visible structures are sparse and widely separated, and we drove and walked through fields and dunes to view them. There was a theater of course—there always is a theater—but a windswept arc of fine white sand filled it from the stage to the upper tiers. It looked spooky, like a sandswept ruin on some distant planet—or at least on the cover of a science fiction novel.

From the top tier of seats we looked west across green-planted fields to where a group of bobbing white scarves enlivened a pastoral painting; village women picking and weeding in front of an almost perfect three-arched Roman gate. Near the long, white sand beach that framed the sea stood a partially excavated yellow stone building, identified as a baths complex. Archeology students from Ankara had cleared a crossroads nearby, revealing perfect marble paving stones. The exposed streets moved away from each other at right angles and then disappeared under abrupt, five-foot-high banks of silt and stones. A thick grove of palm trees grew atop one of these. You could, if you didn't mind wading through some water, walk down these marble streets and stand with your elbow resting on the ground surface beside you—the surface that is now being tilled and weeded by the village women nearby. So what else is hidden? Where do the marble streets lead?

It was a relief, after this sandy puzzle, to attack the mountain home of "Chimaera the unconquerable," a mythical beast with a lion's head and forelegs, a goat's rear, and a snake for a tail. "Homer," says my guidebook, "relates how a certain Bellerophon was ordered by the King of Lycia, Iobates, to kill the Chimaera in atonement for the supposed rape of his daughter Stheneboea, of which he had been wrongly accused. With the help of the winged horse Pegasus, Bellerophon succeeded in this mission, killing the beast from the air by dropping lead into its mouth."

Unfortunately we have no Pegasus to fly us there so after driving through a steep, winding canyon we park at the trailhead and climb the rocky path to where, out of fissures in solid rock, flames leap and burn. It is near dusk, with just a few other people about, and the sight is eerie. The source of the gas is unknown and its composition is unique. It is said that the flames can be extinguished for a short time by water, or if covered with dirt, but the gas eventually re-emerges and re-ignites. Pockets of fire are scattered across the steep rock face and we scramble from one to another, looking for an explanation. Most of the fissures are invisible—there is rock and there is fire. Some spots have small, barely visible flames, others flare like a camper's ideal bonfire. Since this mountain faces the sea the flames can be seen by boats at night, and it's easy to understand how the legends originated. We leave feeling stymied and somewhat awed.

After a delicious dinner and a good night's sleep in Antalya's old town we head to Termessos, a ruin that's been recommended by several friends here as "unbelievable." The weather is sunny, but as we move inland from the coast and up into the mountains white puffy clouds begin to fill the sky. After defeating the Chimaera, Bellerophon was sent to Termessos to fight the Solymians, who are better known by those who know as Pisidians, a warlike people who settled in Anatolia's lake district during the first millennium BC. The Solymians/Pisidians chose a perfect, defensible spot for their city. It is 4,800 feet above sea level, atop a steep mountain that is split on one side by a narrow, rugged valley—the only way up. The site is now surrounded by a national park, one of the few in Turkey.

From the car park we climb a good 20 minutes, following a rocky, narrow path where occasional marble blocks hint at an old roadway. A scatter of ruins lies at the foot of the trail but the real city begins where the valley starts to narrow, and we cross the remains of two widely separated thick stone ramparts. By now we're nearing the top, and the air is cooler. The once distant clouds drift nearby, obscuring and then revealing tantalizing scenes: gray stone pillars outlined against a bright sky, tumbled blocks of stone and marble filling a small canyon with carved and inscribed rubble; high, thick walls topping distant precipices. We round a bend and suddenly, to our left, is a large, almost intact building, its gray facade revealing arched niches where statues must have stood.

Unlike most of Turkey's ruins, which are located near the dry, sunny sea, this one is surrounded by a dense green pine forest. Undergrowth crowds our path, and ivy spreads and clings and drips in picturesque cascades. We agree that it looks like an Indiana Jones kind of ruin, or something out of a Central American jungle. A narrow path leads us to a precipice where a few dozen stone sarcophagi lay open and tossed about—by an earthquake probably, or by gods playing a gruesome game of dice. Beyond this point the mountain drops into folds and crevices, and the distant sea can be glimpsed through clouds.

We retreat back down the path and climb again, across the narrowest end of the valley to the quarry, source of the city's building blocks. Then we separate and go along three different routes, always upward. The size of this city, perched in such an unlikely place, is astounding, and the intact state of the buildings is impressive. Probably this inaccessibility has prevented the looting and destruction that ravaged so many other sites. I don't know how many people lived here but the Greek-style theater is supposed to have held 4,200

Termessos theater

people. It's toward the theater that each of us is headed, hurrying now because the day is slipping away and we have a long drive ahead. I follow overgrown paths past what was a temple to a large gymnasium, its tall, intact walls rising above the surrounding trees. From here it's a short climb over tumbled stone blocks to the well-preserved theater.

I reach it from the highest point in the back; Jennifer is already there, sitting far away on the right side, taking photos. The clouds are lowering and we are slowly being engulfed in fog. Behind the stage is a high wall; behind it the mountain drops into a steep canyon, presenting that distant view of the sea that all ancients seem to have demanded of their theaters. Only now there is no view, only fog. The mist drifts around us, the theater seats drop away from my feet, and we seem to hang in empty, gray space.

It's time to leave, though we haven't seen it all and no one wants to go. We disagree about the route back, finally following Jennifer past deep, elaborate cisterns carved from solid rock (for some reason making me think of the slaves it took to build this place), and back to the path, the second-century Kings Road, that will take us down again. Termessos is the only city, we read, that Alexander the Great failed to conquer (333 BC)—one guidebook says he left in disgust when the city rained rocks onto his army—and in 70 BC it signed a treaty of friendship with Rome that left it free of the jurisdiction of the governor. Apparently someone in Rome knew which battles were worth fighting.

Ray and I plan to go again to Termessos, to see it in bright sunlight and to reach, if we can, the temple that flashed its tantalizing columns through a lacy curtain of fog. Ruins are just so compelling.

A couple of friends

January 20

As part of my slow but continuing quest to comprehend the women of Turkey I sought out Lady Mary Wortley Montagu who came to stay in Constantinople with her ambassador husband in 1717. Lady Mary brought with her the habit of correspondence and an insatiable curiosity. Her husband's status gave her entrée and her willingness to dress in the Turkish style and learn the Turkish language eased her way into the seraglio and harems of upper-class homes.

"The Turkish ladies," she wrote, "are (perhaps) freer than any ladies in the universe, and are the only women in the world that lead a life of uninterrupted pleasure, exempt from cares, their whole time being spent in visiting, bathing, or the agreeable amusement of spending money and inventing new fashions. . . . 'Tis true they have no public places but the *bagnios*, [baths] and there can only be seen by their own sex; however, that is a diversion they take great pleasure in."

Given our prejudicial expectations with regard to Moslem women this is a surprising point of view. But Lady Mary was writing from an 18th century perspective, when women in England were themselves greatly restricted. She admits that Turkish women were compelled to marry, and that producing sons was considered their greatest happiness. Both of these attitudes can still be found, especially in poorer or more traditional households.

I find Lady Mary's opinions interesting, but since neither seraglio nor harems now exist, she is of little practical help. Turning to something more current I open the 1996 U.S. government handbook on Turkey and read, "The 1926 civil code granted women unprecedented legal rights, and in 1934 they received the right to vote and to stand for election. . . . Official state ideology extols the equality of men and women. Intellectually, men tend to accept women as equals, and elite women have been able to achieve high positions in professional careers since the 1960s."

This cheerful prospect dims, however, when the spotlight is turned on lower-class women who, the book states, "are constrained economically and socially." I know this to be true. Lower-class women are generally under the thumb of their mother-in-law until they produce a son or grow older—age eventually granting them the respect that sex never does. Aygul, my upstairs neighbor, appears to get along well with her mother-in-law, but its clear that grandma has the upper hand. (For one thing she has a much louder voice.) Such women have a good deal of authority and influence in the home, despite the constraints, and were I Aygul I would not want to cross her.

Feeling more enlightened but less inspired, my mind drifts back to Constantinople and another Englishwoman who visited there, Agatha Christie. It was Christie's heroine Miss Marple who insisted that all of human nature can be found displayed in village life. What could be simpler then, than to turn to the villages I know best and offer you two profiles of middle-class Turkish women, to draw what conclusions you will.

You have already met Ziya, a smart, funny, petite woman in her early 40s. Because women can retire here after only 15 years of employment, Ziya receives a small pension. "Not enough," she complains, "to live on." To supplement this she works during the long tourist season. When we met her she was managing a bar/restaurant, but this is exhausting work with long hours so the following summer she went to work for a tour company and kept her own office and her own schedule.

Ziya wears her dark, slightly graying hair close-cropped and her clothes are determinedly casual, a fashion that reflects her outlook as well as her politics, for she is an anarchist and proud of it. A photo of Che Guevara is pinned to the bulletin board in her kitchen, and a bigger one hangs in the hall. Ziya's father was a politician; a mayor and then administrator of a region. Perhaps because of this background she is outspoken for a Turk—most of them are circumspect about their political views—and she sometimes makes outrageous statements in her throaty, flat, of-course-it-is-true-why-are-you-surprised voice; the kind of statements that cause you to swing your head around and look again.

Did she really say that?

She did.

One day we met her on the street and she said, "I am going to jail."

"What?" we gasped. "Are you serious?"

"Yes, the *jandarma* are looking for me; you will see me next in jail. You will have to bring me food, the food there is terrible." She ended this melodramatic statement with a wave, said "I must go now," and did.

Her words left us worried and wondering if there was anything we could do, but when we ran into her a few days later everything was back to normal. It was just a misunderstanding over some business matter; taxes or fees had been paid but not recorded. The problem was fixed now. Everything was settled but her residual anger.

Because of her work we didn't see much of her during the tourist months, and when the season ended she went to Istanbul while her ex-husband stayed in her apartment and took care of the dog. But she is back now, adding zest to Göcek's social scene, and when she invited us to dinner to meet her childhood friend, Feride, we naturally accepted.

The evening started quietly, as evenings do when people are unacquainted, but with a glass of wine in our hands and an opinionated anarchist in the apartment it wasn't long before we were in the middle of intense discussions about everything from tourist development on Turkey's coasts, to the current government scandals, the fidelity of women to their friends, the Internet, travel, food, movies, music, men, America, and Hillary Clinton.

The subject of America arose because it always does. Turks usually express a fondness for America and Americans, and Feride had a special interest: her son spent a year in Wisconsin as part of the high school AFS program, and her husband attended Portland State University for two years in the early 70s. U.S. connections are not uncommon here, and the two friends had yet another: they grew up in an Izmir suburb when American troops were attached to the nearby NATO air base. They attended an American school and they listened to American music as teenagers.

"I remember listening to Herman's Hermits," said Feride, "and the Beach Boys—all those groups—on the base radio station. There was an American DJ who took requests, and every day we rushed home from school to call him."

"He was so good," said Ziya. "He was perfect."

"Perfect" is Ziya's pet word. This food is perfect. That book is perfect. Che is perfect.

When she returned from a trip to Istanbul Ziya brought us the perfect gift, a copy of Mina Urgan's 1994 book, *Virginia Woolf*. Of course Mina's award-winning book is in Turkish and neither Ray nor I can read it, but no matter. We will take it to Bodrum when we go this spring, and ask her to autograph it.

We were introduced to Mina in 1987 by one of her former students, our Bodrum landlord. She is shorter than Ziya, older (early 80s), and rounder. But they have much in common. Mina too is a determined leftist. Her father was a member of Atatürk's inner circle and Mina remembers dancing with the great man at a party when she was young.

When we visited in October it had been ten years since we had seen her, and though she has more gray hair now she has changed little. She still spends her summers in Bodrum and her winters in "Stamboul." Summers are defined by the water temperature, for she swims every day, and when the water is too cold to swim—late

Mina Urgan

November this year—she returns to her friends in Istanbul. In '87 she took us to visit one of those friends, the owner of a large wooden *yali* (mansion) on the Bosphorus; a rare treat.

Mina is a retired professor doctor of literature at Istanbul University. Her politics occasionally got her into trouble with the government, and she was once fired and later reinstated because of them. An infection in her vocal chords led to early retirement and writing, including translations of Malory, Fielding, Balzac, Huxley, Graham Greene, and several volumes of Shakespeare into Turkish. She published *Shakespeare and Hamlet* in 1984, a five-volume history of Elizabethan theater between 1986 and 1993, and *Virginia Woolf* in 1994; now she's working on her autobiography.

"Writing keeps me alive," she says. "I love it."

She writes in longhand, filling spiral-bound notebooks while sitting in the tiny courtyard of her old Bodrum house. The house is like Mina: small, smart, stylish, and Turkish. Every room opens onto the courtyard, which is protected from the street by a high wall enclosing a carved wooden door. A bougainvillea climbs over one corner and drops its petals on the paving stones.

The last time we were there we sat talking and drinking tea in the courtyard while Mina's daughter and her English boyfriend carried paint, ladders, and other repair supplies back and forth between us. Their presence went almost unnoticed, so intent in conversation were we.

"Turkey is changing; people only care about getting rich," Mina complains. "We are losing our culture. It's horrible."

This is a refrain we hear frequently from educated, liberal-minded Turks.

Mina, like Ziya, is outspoken on other topics too, and has no hesitation in telling us what we should do with our lives. This is a quality I find refreshing about Turkish women. Unlike most American women they do not speak with passive voices. They do not say, "Well, of course it's not for me to say, but if I were you I would think about doing this . . . . " They say, "Do this!" I like that. Even if I don't want to do it.

Before she read Mina's literary biography of Virginia Woolf, Ziya had not read any of that famous author's books. Now she is working her way through all of them. "Woolf is perfect," she says. We hope one day to introduce her to Mina. We know she will say, "Mina is perfect" too.

Göcek in winter

January 28

Much to our surprise, we're discovering that Göcek is a busy place in winter. This has nothing to do with the number of people in town or with daily invitations to Göcek's social extravaganzas. This busyness evokes the sound of falling rocks and the rumble of cement mixers; it has to do with building. Like many Turkish towns on the Aegean and Mediterranean coasts, Göcek has strict limits on when in-town construction is permitted. It is certainly not allowed while tourists are around, so that leaves winter—November through April.

These months of change have exposed a startling transience that suggests latent nomadic instincts. It's apparently easy to tear down and build up again. The impermanence of the building blocks themselves—fragile, hollow, red-clay bricks and mixed-at-the-site concrete—may have something to do with it. At any rate, in the private sector at least, the Turks seem capable of redesigning and re-constructing everything from a building facade to the totality of their businesses in a very short time.

It isn't just buildings that are being revamped either. Several business owners are using the winter break to computerize their operations. Ilhan recently installed a computer system in his small grocery store, and it includes a hand-held optical scanner for the bar codes that are in use even here. His computer is now linked by mo-dem to the wholesaler in Dalaman and his prices are automatically updated from there. No more memorization, except for the village olive oil and other local products. Ilhan loves his computer but so far he's the only one who knows how to operate it. His father, he tells us sadly in English that's on a par with our Turkish, is much too old to learn computing skills. When we start to protest he adds, with a shrug of his shoulders, "he's 740."

Outside Ilhan's grocery a ditch runs the full length of main street. It's been there about a month now, and adjacent businesses have placed boards across it for the benefit of their customers. The ditch represents one of the *belediye's* (the municipal government's) major winter projects—a new water system. Ditches have appeared in every street in town, hindering traffic for at least a month. (The mayor's street, we noticed, was only ditch-encumbered for a couple of days.) Our house was surrounded by criss-crossing ditches for over two months, and a trip to the market was like threading through a maze. Only one ditch now remains, however, and we cross it on a plank that Ray threw across.

The *belediye* is an ardent lover of construction projects but, as we've said before, it has a hard time completing tasks; it needs firm discipline and should never be allowed out with a back hoe. In addition to the ditch project, one crew is working to extend the paved, waterfront promenade a half kilometer to the west, and another is replacing old wooden power poles with new concrete ones. At the east end of the promenade a block-long stretch of old village houses was recently torn down to make way for another municipal marina. A major new road is being worked on nearby, and the hill next door continues to serve as a quarry, satisfying the *belediye's* voracious appetite for rock. Finally, the new covered market that was under construction when we arrived—a simple structure consisting of a concrete floor, steel posts and corrugated roof—is still under construction. All this in a village of fewer than 500 people. The only element in Göcek that doesn't seem to be under construction is its population, unless you count the pregnancies in town.

One notable exception in this rush for change is Mr. Dim, who is spending the winter much like the summer, sitting at his large, carved wooden desk, overseeing his empire. To keep warm, he has brought in a gas stove like ours, except that the exhaust pipe ends a foot above the stove top and vents straight into the store. But that's all right because the store's front door is always open.

Aside from the construction you could say, if you were forced to, that not much is happening in Göcek. On sunny days you can find people lunching outside at the Çan or the Nanai, but not much else is open and there is little to do or spend money on. There are only three open restaurants and as many cafes, and each offers just one or two entrees. There are six open "supermarkets" and their contents together might fill one medium-sized 7–11. And there's a chandler for the die-hard yachties who refuse to go away.

But we can still buy our *Turkish Daily News* or an occasional *Newsweek* at the little newsstand, and Nurhan's stationery store supplies us with pens and paper and photocopy services. If we crave entertainment we can find it at the music shop, or we can borrow a book or video from an English-speaking friend. The Arçelik dealer is open in case our washing machine breaks down, and if we needed building supplies we could certainly find plenty. And of course the outdoor *pazar* sets up every Sunday. As you can see, we've everything we need, and we're very, very busy.

The Tost of the Town: A review

February 3

The winter closing of most Göcek restaurants has left your intrepid reporters with few reviewing choices. However, much to our surprise, one of the local "bests," the village-run Belediye Cafe, remains open. Yes, most of the pleasant outdoor tables have been moved inside a jerry-built, barn-like structure, but the same silent, bureaucratic staff still serves the same limited menu to the few hardy adventurers who can't resist the outdoor tables.

Your reporters therefore took advantage of a sunny day recently to return to our familiar table (no anonymity possible here) and order our old lunch standby, *tost*. The fact that this is the only item on the menu had absolutely no bearing on our decision. We would have ordered it anyway.

Turkish *tost* is made using a half loaf of traditional bread (unsliced, fat baguettes, three- or four-inches high and 15 inches long) slit long-ways down the middle and filled with cheese, beef sausage, and a red sauce resembling ketchup. After the bread is layered with these ingredients it is placed in a machine that heats and flattens it to a thickness of less than a half-inch. The thin, stiff remains are *tost*.

The waiter, not a charming and handsome young man from the provinces (CHYMFP), but a local man, approached the table as we sat down and showed remarkable cachet when we ordered, *"iki Fanta, iki tost, lütfen."* As he ambled away with our order we noted that the tablecloth was looking a bit disreputable, but we brushed the crumbs away and settled ourselves in the purple plastic chairs to gaze seaward. It wasn't long before our order appeared: two glasses of orange drink and two orders of *tost* wrapped in white paper. The waiter retired to the kitchen TV and we were left with only a few hungry cats for company.

Tost is nothing if not chewy so we munched and drank and munched and drank, carefully judging the texture and flavor and giving our jaws a good workout as we basked in the winter sun. The once-crowded *belediye* pier, now with only a few fishing dories alongside, stretched away in front of us leaving an unhindered view of the dark green islands to the south.

Even a local waiter knows that leaving dirty dishes in front of a diner is bad manners, so we had scarcely set our empty drink glasses on the table before our waiter pulled himself from the *futbol* match and swept them away in a grand gesture. Nothing to complain about there.

Bereft of dishes but with no place to go, we stretched out our legs and sat longer in the sun, watching the waves lap against the pier. Then, offering our last few bits of *tost*—judged excellent—to the cats, we called for the check, paid, and ambled down the promenade, full and content.

The sound of a different drummer

February 6

The month of Ramadan, when good Moslems go without food, liquid, sex, or cigarettes from sunup to sundown, ends this weekend, and that makes us happy. Not because we've been fasting, which in fact might have done us some good, but because Ramadan (or Ramazan as the Turks call it) brought with it an unanticipated irritant. Every morning around 3:30 a.m. we are awakened by the slow thud thud thud! thud thud thud! of a strange, hollow-sounding drum. This drumbeat, the work of a strolling village employee, is the signal for good Moslem women to get up and cook breakfast so the family can eat before daybreak. In our building this means that the drumbeat is inevitably followed by the sound of shuffling footsteps overhead, and the occasional slamming of doors. (For religious purposes, sunup and sundown are when one can distinguish—or no longer distinguish—a white thread from a black one.)

I can't find anything in our copy of the Koran that decrees drum beating for Ramazan and presumably most people have alarm clocks these days, but the habit seems firmly ensconced. It's probably an Arabic tradition and we know it has been going on since at least 1894 because the French diarist Pierre Loti, writing about his trek by camel across the Sinai desert in *The Desert,* describes this drum, "sending its slow and hollow beat down the dark oasis pathways." This is a lovely image, but it fails to reflect our feelings when the drum is being beat beat beaten outside the window in the middle of the night. I would like to see one of these traditional noisemakers, but the idea of getting up at 3:30 a.m. to track down the performer has not been compelling enough. If we lived in a city we would undoubtedly also hear the cannon fire or other loud boom signaling sundown and the end of the day's fasting.

The range of religious devotion varies here in Turkey, as it does at home. Some take it seriously, others ignore it completely, and the majority fall somewhere in between. Göcek is not a very religious village, an observation that's confirmed by our local Turkish friends, one of whom declares that even the hodja—the local religious leader—drinks alcohol. Certainly not everyone here is fasting. Nevertheless we have noticed some behavioral changes: daily attendance at the mosque has increased, and women are attending in the evenings. Some of the village women have modified their scarves and are covering their heads more completely. The people who are fasting look more and more tired, and tempers occasionally flare. Everyone is looking forward to Ramazan's end, and to the three days of feasting, visiting, and celebrating that mark it.

Nursel, the young woman who comes to our apartment twice a week for help with her English, tells me that fasting during Ramazan is good for the body because it gives one's insides time to rest. She's a modern young woman who works at a yacht service and takes correspondence classes in economics from the university in Muğla. This year at least, her fasting is limited to weekends. She also explains that the month-long period is more than just a fast. It is a time for getting in touch with family and friends who live far away, and a period devoted to re-evaluation and contemplation.

On Air, a monthly publication of the BBC, reflects this view, reporting that the fast is believed by Moslems to promote spiritual well-being. Ramazan, it says, "teaches self-discipline. It reminds one of human frailty and dependence upon God, but above all it fosters compassion, for only the hungry know what hunger really is."

It's been interesting for us to follow, if only peripherally, the practice of fasting and observance during this holy month. Islam is so much in the news, and so much of that news is negative, that the words "Islam" and "Moslem" raise the specter of fear in western hearts. I am not a religious person, and if I were I would not be a Moslem. But this month reminds us that we live surrounded by people who are Moslem, and they are not radical, intolerant extremists. They are hospitable, helpful, friendly, and compassionate. Thankfully, the 3:30 a.m. drum beating will soon cease; the stereotyping and derogation will probably not.

The massage

Ray writes: February 10

I took a morning *dolmuş* on Tuesday from the petrol station to Fethiye by myself to wander around and peer into shops and people-watch and take a few colorful photographs.

After an excellent lunch of "chickie bobs" (87¢) I was walking past a small market to take a photo of a Lycian tomb which had been standing in the middle of a nearby street for 2,000 years or so and a man caught up with me and asked if I spoke English. "A little" I said. Amazingly it was someone who had given us directions on a hot and humid day last summer .

Well he asked me if I would like a cup of *çay*. "Apple *çay* lemon *çay* . . ." and not to be rude I accepted his hospitality and said "Why not?" So we walked back to the little market and he placed a small wooden table and some chairs in the street in the sun. Then we chatted for a while about his family he has a wife and seven children and he mentioned how little money he has and he told me that he speaks Française and Allaman and English and Italiano and worked in a Turkish bath and was a masseur for ten years and did I want one. Well assuming he meant a massage I politely said no but he said just a small one on my head and not to be rude I accepted his hospitality and said "Why not?" Then he said he had to get his cream. "Cream?" I asked "for a small massage of the head?" Then while his two friends watched and while I this somewhat conspicuous American sat at the little wooden table in the sun on the street in Fethiye he told me that my outer shirt must come off. So I took it off and then he put some cream from a tube on my arms and my forehead.

Fortunately I had the foresight to ask him what my massage was going to cost and he gave the standard Turkish reply "Money no problem." So I replied back to him I'm glad that money is no problem but don't massage me for more than *iki yuz* (TL200,000) worth. After a somewhat greasy two-minute massage his boss the market owner came over and sat down and as I complimented the masseur on his fine hands he (the masseur) thought *bes yuz* (TL500,000) would be an appropriate amount for a person of my standing—or sitting in this case—to pay for his skilled work. Two times I had to firmly remind him that I ordered an *iki yuz* massage and he finally accepted these terms mostly I think because his boss was there and then we departed amiably as he invited me back again for a big massage.

Then on my walk to the big *otogar* to find a midibus back to Göcek I stopped to take a colorful photo and a man turned to me and said "Good photos . . ."

And that's another story.

The Lycian tomb

In the land of touchy-feely

Ray writes: February 14

With the ending of Ramadan and the beginning of the three-day Moslem *Eid al-Fitr* holiday, Göcek came alive last week. Businesses, with the exception of restaurants and markets, closed. The post office, not wanting to be outdone, closed for four days. There was a feeling of festivity in the air, buoyed by sunny, 70-degree weather. Buses from as far away as Istanbul brought Turkish tourists into town for part of the day, then carried them off to other destinations. Families dressed in their finest—as many as four generations—filled the restaurants and strolled the promenade and greeted friends by shaking hands, hugging, and kissing one another on the cheek. (Respect for one's elders is shown by kissing the back of the elder's hand, then raising it to touch your forehead. Since no one did this to me I figure I haven't yet crossed the abyss.)

Children went from house to house and to businesses collecting small amounts of candy and the lira equivalent of five or ten cents. In Ilhan's market a lad about seven years old came in, collected his candy and solemnly shook hands with everyone in the store before leaving. Turkey is a "touchy-feely" country and I must admit I was somewhat taken aback the first time I saw men kissing, or walking arm in arm, and especially seeing two uniformed Turkish soldiers walking hand in hand. And this is a fierce army. So much for my hangups; as we've said many times: different country, different customs.

With *Eid al-Fitr* behind us I eagerly looked forward to Valentine's day. In Istanbul there were many choices for Valentine lovers. At the Swissotel on the Bosphorus, for TL 22,000,000 ($190), you could have a room with a view, champagne, a "Just for Two" dinner starting with terrine of marinated and smoked salmon with celerial and caviar cream sauce, veal medallions, and quail breast served with artichoke and mushroom cream, ending with Valrone chocolate mousse, petit fours and coffee, and if the lovers happened to be hungry the next morning, breakfast.

At the Polat Renaissance Istanbul Hotel, "every lady will receive a rose and the gentlemen a nice chocolate bag. Lovers may enjoy a romantic candlelight atmosphere in Polat Mangal Restaurant. The Fasil Music will accompany your dinner and the roses and chocolate bags will be also offered. You may also enjoy Special Valentine's Buffet in a romantic Germanic atmosphere at Bier Stube. Ring (0 212) 663 1700."

After all that, there's still another bayram (holiday) to come. Forty days after *Eid al-Fitr* it's *Kurban bayram,* the Feast of Sacrifice, when those who can afford it slaughter a ram and share the meat with the poor. This was graphically demonstrated when Ilhan drew his forefinger slowly across his throat. If I were a sheep or a goat I'd book into the Swissotel for that one.

As the world turns

One of the things we like best about our year without work is having time to feel the earth turning beneath our feet. It helps, of course, that the sky is usually clear, for this makes the sun's location easier to monitor and the turning easier to gauge. But even if the sun had shone every day in Oregon, I would not have been able to tell you when it would cast what shadows on my floor, or exactly where on the horizon it would set. Who had time for that?

Now, we do. Life is slow here, and nature is a close partner in our daily dance. The moon shines unhindered through our bedroom windows and I'm aware of its movement across the star-filled sky. I see the sun rise each day, first a little further south, now a little further north along the mountainous ridge to the east, and I watch it set over the quarried hill to the west. I see the shadows on the floor lengthen and shorten again as Earth spins through its long journey around the sun. I can almost measure its movement in inches, standing at the kitchen window, watching the sun settle each evening through the pine trees.

The circling earth influences behavior—ours and others'. This fall bee hives sprouted overnight in nearby pine forests. I do not know where the bees lived beforehand, but they've been busy in their boxes and jars of "bee's milk" are now being sold around town. The tenderizing slapping of an octopus on the stone quay is another seasonal indicator. The octopi move into shallower, warmer waters in winter and the first one we saw was clinging to a rock a few feet off the Club Marina pier. A Turk spotted it too, and quicker than you could say, "get your spear-gun there's an octopus" he had the creature pierced and was carrying it off to dinner.

We are close to our sources of sustenance here, and conscious of the seasons' influence on our diet. With rare exceptions, our produce is local: watermelons give way to mandarins which give way to mushrooms. Peaches turn into lemons and lettuce into cauliflower. Cabbage and leeks could not be found in July, yet suddenly in October there they are. Coke bottles full of local olive oil sprouted after the harvest in mid-November, and last week we saw the first, spring-heralding strawberries. As the produce changes so do our menus and our diet and, one presumes, our bodies. A few items, like tomatoes, do grow year round in nearby hothouses. Still, the sense of seasonal change and planetary circling is strong.

It can also be noisy. The frogs that live in the irrigation ditch beside the house are at it again. They kept us awake when we first arrived, strangers to the sounds and colors of Göcek. We weren't even sure what they were at first, they didn't sound like the frogs we knew. They sounded like wild animals, snuffling through the undergrowth, waiting to pounce on our soft, citified selves. I'm embarrassed to admit that it was weeks before we recognized them for what they are. Their voices disappeared during the coldest months, but they are back now, chirping and growling and clucking and croaking like tattletale scandalmongers. We hear them. We know what they are. We know they are there. We even like them.

One thing that doesn't change much is the foliage. Neither eucalyptus nor pines nor olive trees lose their leaves. There are a few oaks and maples about, but not within our daily range of vision. Nor do the flowers change much. We see Helen's bougainvillea, our geraniums, others' hibiscus all continually blooming. Still, it rains occasionally, the air is cooler, and we watch from the promenade as the sea chops and rolls in a stiffer breeze. At home in Oregon the seasons are more marked and more beautiful, but I'm happy for now to accept these milder reminders of change.

Two acquaintances of ours, Carol and Annie, have just had first babies; both boys, a week apart. This is life cycling on a grand scale. The change from carefree young woman to mother was quick and complete, and Annie fussed and fumed when a local construction worker picked up 12-day-old William and planted a kiss on his cheek.

"What if he had tuberculosis?" she moans, while an unconcerned William settles into sleep on her shoulder.

Ray and I watch these transformations with bemused tolerance, happy to be free of that kind of worry and responsibility. Let those particular planets circle without us for now. We go home to a cup of coffee, to watching the sunlight crawl across the floor, to seeing the Earth turning beneath our feet.

The hives that bring us bee's milk.

Trouble in paradise

Ray writes: March 3

When life in Göcek becomes too comfortable and everything runs smoothly, we get nervous. This week the tranquillity was broken when the *belediye* again worked on the village water system. For most of the week the tap has been delivering blasts of half-water, half-air. The pipes knock, the shower spits, the toilet and the hot water heater burp loudly. Throughout the building water-related secrets are shared with all.

The electricity, hearing about the problems of the water, shut off three times and Thursday evening I found myself writing by candlelight. It was nice until the electricity returned and the ambiance was lost. We heat and cook using tanks of propane gas, our radio is battery powered and candles are cheap, so being without electricity for short periods isn't a hardship.

Then Compuserve decided to take a six day holiday—trouble in the telephone lines. This creates the most anxiety for us because email is our primary method of communicating with the outside world. We always wonder if and when it will return. Then on Saturday, as mysteriously as it went down, it came back up.

Life goes on, slow and almost steady, a few bumps here and there; but next week we begin praying to Allah that the *belediye* stays out of the propane business.

SPRING

Look, listen, live

March 10

There's a microwave oven in the tree outside our window. I can't see it, but the beeping sound I hear must mean it's finished cooking and I wish whoever owns it would come and collect it; it's driving me crazy. Maybe it's a bird; it seems to move from tree to tree and I don't think microwave ovens do that. But birds don't sound like that either, do they?

There are other sounds floating through the window this sunny afternoon. The *belediye's* red, rusting c.1928 Austin Western grader, the one with the rusting levers, the doorless, almost floorless cab, and the missing windows, is putt-putting somewhere on the other side of the little river. Its engine has a unique pitch so we always know when it's around. One of these days it's going to clank clatter collapse onto its bald-tired wheels and everyone in the village will gather round to mourn, and then they'll carry away the bones and reuse them.

Not far from where the grader is working there's a soccer field, and I can hear the yells and hoots of children kicking a soccer ball around. *Futbol* is the number one sport here, and there's almost always a pickup game going on somewhere in town. This particular field is used every afternoon; sometimes it's a group from school and there are organized games, other times it's just boys booting a ball.

The noises they make are happy ones though, and I know when I hear them that it's time to stop what I'm doing and think about fixing dinner; or maybe tell Ray to think about fixing dinner.

When the wind is right the sounds of the highway come through the window too. Turks love to toot their horns, which often play more than one note. If I paid closer attention to the various tunes I could no doubt tell you when the *dolmuş* passes a certain house, when the Izmir bus goes by the benzene station, and when that friend of the woman who lives on the corner goes to Fethiye. After honking, the most predominant traffic noise is the infamous, high-pitched buzz of motorbikes that pierces glass, clay bricks, and fillings. Their number is legion. We see ancient motorbikes and motorcycles kept running with nothing but baling wire and super glue and appeals to Allah. Nothing mechanical ever seems to be junked here, it gets rebuilt and repainted and repaired and resold and recycled and redeemed.

The *belediye* must be testing new mosquito-killing equipment, for there goes a man carrying something that looks like a leaf blower and roars like only a two-cylinder engine without a muffler can, spitting yards and yards of oily blue smoke and, probably, insecticide. He's following the road next to the river and three boys are chasing along behind, breathing in the fumes and eager to see what's what. Göcek's regular bug machine is an old beat-up pickup with a motor on the back and a big drum filled with something smelly, and it roars down every road in town about once a week during mosquito season. This occasionally causes consternation on the waterfront, as we witnessed one evening last summer. It was a busy Saturday night and the restaurant tables lining the sidewalks and the promenade were full of diners enjoying the balmy evening. Then down the main street, straight through the pedestrians and feet away from scores of diners, comes the bug machine, belching noise and billowing fumes. The tourists grabbed napkins to cover their faces or their food, and a few aimed hard looks at the driver. But this is Turkey after all. Most of us shrugged and kept on eating.

Maybe the warming sun is bringing all these people out; there's a peddler now, calling out his wares. He's the second I've seen in as many days. They've suddenly appeared from nowhere, selling blue, red, and yellow plastic buckets, basins and baskets from off their backs. He pauses for a minute and looks up at the window, but I shake my head no and he turns, to saunter back toward the village.

Most of the noises that drift through our afternoon windows are pleasant; the mooing of cows, the clucking of chickens, the pad, pad, swish, swish of grandma's feet moving through the garden below. I like to stay cognizant of grandma's whereabouts (her ever-present cigarette helps), because she has a habit of startling me with incredibly resonant screeches at unexpected moments. Her voice has a high-pitched, glass-breaking tone that would shame a banshee, and when she lets go everyone within a half-mile hears. One of our friends calls these shrieks "barnyard hollers," and says all peasant women develop them to communicate over long distances. I would guess it works.

There's the afternoon prayer call. The *müezzin* sounds stronger now than he did this morning; I was afraid he was coming down with something. I am turning into a regular village busybody, sitting here at the window. But this is one of the things I came to Turkey for—to feel at home with sights and sounds different from those we left behind. And except for the bird that sounds like a microwave oven, I think I'm beginning to succeed.

A close shave

Throughout our stay in Göcek we'd made it a habit to walk up the hill to the spring and bring back plastic jerry cans filled with spring water. Our tap water was perfectly okay to drink, but with the continuing construction in the hills above our house it sometimes ran muddy or disappeared altogether. This habit of drinking spring water served us well until an evening in March.

Earlier in the day Ray had noticed a scum developing on the inside of one of the water jugs. He poured in a mixture of water and purifying bleach (known by the brand name Axion) and unthinkingly left it to soak on the kitchen counter. You probably won't be surprised to learn that on his way to bed that night he stopped and poured a glass of water. It wasn't until he had the mixture in his mouth that he realized he'd poured it from the wrong jug.

He managed to spit most of it out, but not before enough had been swallowed to seriously frighten us. He quickly drank lots of fresh water, tried to vomit, decided that wasn't a good idea, and drank more water. Then he drank milk. Then we called Carol, who lives nearby and speaks English and Turkish, and told her what happened. She called the village doctor, who told us to report to the clinic, where he wrote a prescription for two neutralizing medicines. Then the doctor called the pharmacist. About 11:30 p.m. the pharmacist met us at his little shop on main street and watched carefully as Ray downed his medicine.

The next day our hero felt foolish but fine, except for a slight burning sensation in his mouth and throat. The story made the rounds though, and for a few days he was known around town as Axion Man.

Ray writes: March 17

As acculturated as I must be after eight months in Türkiye, from time to time I still see things that leave me amazed. Wednesday I drove to Ortaca in Bob and Helen's rental car to pick up a rug for their boat. (To digress, I'm feeling decadent today because for the first time in eight months I drove a car to a store to buy some groceries).

I love going to Ortaca, it's a solid Turkish town of about 15,000 people with few-to-no tourists and little spoken English. The *centrum* is a tight collection of businesses, near a sizable *otogar*. The streets are abuzz with activity; tractors, trucks, motorcycles (some with sidecars), mopeds, cars, mini-buses, big-buses, pushcarts, goats, chickens and people, all going in every direction. Kiosks and vendors abound. I love to walk around, peer into shops, try my taxi Turkish, have lunch, go to the *pazar* and walk the neighborhoods. This is ethnic at ethnic's best.

This day I dropped in on the *berber* for a shave. Three lads in their early teens led me to the *berber* chair and directed me to sit and lean my head back on the rest. For the next three minutes I was lathered to an incredible pitch by the young maestro (smartly clad in a white pharmacist's jacket), as his eager and curious assistants looked on. The young *berber* then honed his straight razor on a wide leather strap, and with the skill of an open-heart surgeon shaved me not once, but twice.

The shave completed, an assistant handed the *berber* steel forceps that held a cotton ball at their tip. After dipping the cotton in an alcohol solution he ignited it and to my surprise, lightly touched the flaming ball to the inside of each of my ears. Pure genius, I thought, no more scissor cuts removing that nasty, unwanted hair. After the smoke cleared he applied hot steaming towels to my face,

covering my eyes, and the massage began. The *berber* worked on
my neck and shoulders as his assistants stepped in to massage my
arms and hands. Then came lavish quantities of cologne, followed
by aftershave and clouds of talc. A final spray of yet another cologne
completed my toilet. Exhausted but unscathed, I paid the *berber*
TL100,000 (80¢) plus a tip, and headed for lunch.

A few doors down from the *berber* I found a *pide saluno* (four
tables and three employees). These are simple restaurants offering a
simple menu—*pide*. *Pide* is best described as an elongated, thin pizza
with minced meat and
parsley spread on top.
The sides are folded
over, leaving the meat
exposed. It's baked
in a wood-fired oven,
cut into strips and
topped with a hunk of
butter. *Pide* is served
with hot, dried pep-
pers. Tea and water

are available; my coke was brought from a nearby grocery. *Pide* and
Coke—TL 200,000 ($1.60).

After lunch I headed for the main street. Waiting to cross, I
watched an old car pass slowly in front of me from right to left. A
second look confirmed my surprised first impression: from the car's
back seat a black cow was gazing forlornly out at me through the
rear window. My day was made.

Song of Susurlik

March 24

We've been trying to keep politics out of our reports but it seems only fair to let you in on the spectacle. Watching Turkish politics is like watching a good opera. The plot is obscure, the performers dramatic, the action noisy, and the outcome predictable. Well, usually predictable.

(Caveat: My primary source is the *Turkish Daily News*. Since I often have trouble deciphering their English syntax, let alone the subtleties of Turkish politics, what follows is a semi-educated guess.)

The action begins offstage, in November, when a car is hit by a bus. The car is carrying a former deputy police chief of Istanbul, a member of parliament and leader of a pro-Kurdish clan, an internationally-sought killer, and a former model. All but the member of parliament die in the crash, and questions are naturally asked about why these particular people were together in a car that also contained a hidden arsenal of sophisticated weapons, fake ID cards, and fake license plates. This event is known as the Susurlik incident.

The Susurlik incident revealed mafia and underworld links to high-ranking government officials, cover-ups by same, murder, corruption in the police department, corruption in the government, connections between drug running and the PKK, etc. This delighted the daily papers, giving them plenty of opportunities for lurid headlines. One full-page article a few weeks ago was headlined, "Is Tansu Çiller the Godmother?" (Tansu Çillar was prime minister at the time.) Susurlik is still under investigation.

Concurrent with Susurlik is the saga of Tansu Çiller, (pronounced Chill-ar) the former prime minister, head of the True Path party (DYP), and now foreign minister in a coalition government with the Refah party (RP), led by Islamist Necmettin Erbakan. Remember these names please. When Çiller was prime minister she was hostile to the RP, which brought several charges of corruption against her. After an election last winter that produced no clear majority, Çiller and the DYP agreed to form a coalition government with Erbakan and the RP, if they would support her against the very charges they had originally brought. The RP, anxious for power and with only 21 percent of the vote, agreed, thereby effectively disowning its campaign promise of a cleaner government. Erbakan was named prime minister and Çiller became the deputy prime minister and foreign minister. Both move to center stage right.

Charges of corruption by government officials must be heard by the Supreme Court, but first they must be referred to the court by a parliamentary vote. With the DYP and the RP voting together, as they promised they would, all the corruption charges against Çiller were defeated by slim margins, the final vote taken last week. Now that she is free of the weight of these charges and no longer beholden to the RP, what will she do? That's a good question.

It's a good question because the RP is in trouble with the army and so is Çiller, but not so much.

The RP contains a few moderate members and many radical members whose goal is nothing less than the destruction of Turkey's secular state and the creation of an Islamic one. To this end they eased some restrictions on government and religious separation, encouraged the building of more religious schools, built more mosques (they want to put a big one in Taksim Square in Istanbul) and tried to lift the ban on the wearing of headscarves by students and public employees. The headscarf issue may sound silly, but in fact it carries implications far beyond that humble symbol.

Enter, stage right, the Iranian ambassador, Muhammed Reza Bagheri. On February 1 Bagheri spoke at a Jerusalem Day rally given by the (RP) mayor of an Ankara suburb, Sincan. The rally was in support of the Palestinians. [The stage is covered with waving banners. A chorus of women—heads covered—stands center right mouthing anti-Israeli slogans as the orchestra sounds clashing cymbals.]

The ambassador made "insolent and provocative" statements ("God will punish those who sign agreements with the United States and Israel"), and outraged the secular, democratic majority that is strongly supported by the Turkish army that now enters stage left, driving tanks through Sincan in a show of force and hinting that it will step in if the fundamentalists don't watch their step.

At this point there is much talk about the "darkness and disaster the RP is carrying Turkey toward" and the newspapers report rumors of coups, rumors of government breakdowns, of coalition meltdowns, and of disaster in general. After days of uproar the mayor of Sincan resigns and the Iranian ambassador and consul-general are expelled. Iran in return ousts two Turkish diplomats who exit stage left.

February 1 also marks the beginning of a grassroots movement called the One Minute's Darkness for Enlightenment Campaign, that asks people to turn off the lights in their homes for one minute at 9 p.m. each evening. This campaign against the corruption revealed in the Susurlik incident spreads rapidly. Offstage, citizens gather on the streets with candles, and the inevitable scuffles with police occur. Later the campaign takes on the added dimension of a pro-secular demonstration.

In mid-February President Demirel reportedly sends a letter to Prime Minister Erbakan expressing concern over the Islamist tendencies in the government. Erbakan denies receiving such a letter. With Çiller scheming behind the scenery there are calls by the heads of other parties, (the YP, the DP, the DSP, etc.) for censure motions and new elections. The National Security Council (MGK) then takes center stage, calling for a meeting to be held February 28. The MGK is a "liaison platform for top state, government, and military officials." The military is the country's most powerful supporter of Atatürk's "six arrows" (secularism, republicanism, populism, etatism, reformism, and nationalism), that represent his founding vision of modern Turkey. In following its perceived mission to safeguard this heritage the army has intervened three times: 1960, 1971, and 1980.

The MGK meeting lasts all day and into the night. The army presents the government with a 20-point list of anti-fundamentalist measures and strongly suggests that Erbakan sign it. Included are the limitation of clerical schools, the banning of Muslim sects, and limitation of financial support to the RP from Islamist associations abroad. After three days of hedging, and after a strong declaration that the military has no right to impose legislation, he signs. (Or does he? Later reports vary.)

His signature does not mark the end, however. Now there are calls for the parliament to discuss the 20 points—something that has never been done with regard to an MGK decision. Everyone is maneuvering to hold on to power, or to cast out those who have power. So far the army has said it will hold off, that the democratic system should be given time to work. But there are those—many here in Göcek—who hope the army will take over. There is a good deal of fear here concerning the fundamentalist right. The specter of the Iranian revolution lingers, hanging like a cloudy wisp near the stage-door entrance.

If this were a real opera it might end with Erbakan dueling the MGK and dying in Çiller's arms, after which she could unmask to reveal she's really the leader of the opposition. There's no shortage of plot twists and possible outcomes; like Constantinople before her, Ankara's a wealth of potential political potboilers. My real concern is that we'll have to leave Turkey before the final curtain.

To market, to market

Turkish time

March 31

Turkey went on daylight saving time this weekend. This won't affect us much since our appointments are few and far between, but since we recently renewed our visas for our fourth and final quarter here, the movement of time is apparent, and the change seems somehow appropriate.

Time is a loose construct in this country, and clocks are not closely watched. Most people and some businesses operate on "Turkish time." That means nothing occurs when it is scheduled to occur, and everything takes longer than expected. New arrivals soon become aware of this different construct; the fortunate adapt quickly and as quickly perceive the drawbacks (some events occur earlier than scheduled) and the benefits (no one is ever late). When living with Turkish time one word is essential, and it soon becomes part of every foreigner's vocabulary: yavaş. Slowly.

Because we adapted many months ago it was no surprise last week to be told to be at the ferry office at 8:30 a.m. for our 9 o'clock crossing to Kos, only to wait in a ragged line for 40 minutes until the customs official ambled up and unlocked his dusty little office, shoved open the ill-fitting sliding window, carefully replaced the date on his heavy, official stamp, and just as carefully scrutinized each face and passport photo. When a tourist with a watch began to roll his eyes and complain of all this sluggishness, I heard the English expat in line ahead of me mutter complacently, "Yavaş, yavaş."

This still being the off season, the ferry's principal cargo was a little group of expats traveling to Greece to renew three-month visas. Among them were two English women from Fethiye, three young women, English and German, who work in Bodrum; and us. One of the Fethiye women had her car on board because according to Turkish regulations a car brought into Turkey must leave the country every three months. And every year the car must stay out for six months. These kinds of regulations, which sometimes seem to change from place to place and official to official, make life difficult for foreigners, but apparently not so difficult as to force them away from Turkey. The woman with the car has lived here eight years and—despite her complaints—loves it.

This every-three-month-trek to Greece has become so routine that for a change of pace we stayed two nights in Bodrum at the Manastir, a nice three- or four-star hotel, depending on which piece of the hotel's literature you are looking at. We made the trip to Bodrum in a well-used midibus and the four-hour ride was rough. It was brightened, though, by the spring flowers that grow daily more numerous, and so was not unpleasant. There were the usual roadside entertainments—unique, motorized people-movers (descriptions fail me); grazing donkeys, horses, cows, and herds of black goats; forest workers from the east, the women with covered heads and hidden faces; a line of men sowing seeds by hand from big, shallow baskets; and two village women having lunch in a spring-green field, their long, colorful skirts billowing around them where they sat.

My favorite part of this now familiar drive is west of Muğla, where rock walls and terraced plots cover every acre of the scrabbly, steep hills. Some walls are so ancient and decayed their tracks are barely discernible; others are well-tended and newly mended.

I love these walls; they are history made solid and represent a continuity that is oddly reassuring. As we bounced along through the mountains I thought about the comet crossing overhead, and concluded that these gray rock walls would have looked much the same had I passed through with Hale-Bopp 4,000 years ago. There was a settlement at Troy even then, and if people were also here they were surely doing what they do now: building and mending rock walls, tending their olive trees and goats, hauling water, gossiping with friends, and having their lunch in spring-green fields. The past is the present is the future. Yavaş, yavaş.

Taking the morning ferry from Bodrum to Kos and returning in the afternoon gives us enough time to pick up some bacon and salami for Rick and Beverly, and the pork chops that Ray says he is craving and I say he doesn't need. The sun is out so we find an outdoor table and order our favorite gyros sandwich and a half-bottle of retsina. The American family sitting at the table behind me are still on American time. They arrive after we do, gobble their meal, and depart while we're still sitting, enjoying the sun. I want to turn around and say, "slowly, slowly," but I know their compulsion so I keep my mouth shut. We, however, congratulate ourselves on our accomplishment—for surely it is one—and go for a last stroll around town before heading for the 3 p.m. ferry.

When we get there we find most of the passengers are the same ones who crossed with us in the morning. The two tourists who came across to visit Hippocrates' Asklepion are already on the upper deck enjoying the sun, the two Fethiye women are sitting in the car, which is back aboard, and the three young women are tucked inside the cabin, smoking and gossiping. And when the ferry leaves the dock ten minutes early not a head turns in concern, not a voice is raised in protest. We're all already back on Turkish time.

Who, me?

Ray writes: April 3

Last July, sometime during my second swim in the Mediterranean, the brown coloring I had added to my hair back home was washed away by the salt water. The chemical tan followed, but was soon replaced by an authentic bronze glow.

When I stepped off the midibus in Bodrum last Tuesday, a little more gray and infinitely more relaxed, I watched as the assistant driver carefully removed our bags from the storage compartment. Then, without warning, he took my right hand as if to shake it, but instead kissed the back of it and touched it to his forehead. This gesture, which shows the greatest respect for the aged, left me horrified, as this was obviously a case of mistaken identity.

The experience made my trip to Kos even more meaningful; I was entering the land of Grecian Formula, where time could again be held in abeyance. At least, until another swim in the Mediterranean.

Supermarket sheep

April 19

I learned how to sacrifice a goat on Friday. It was the first day of the four-day Feast of the Sacrifice (Kurban bayram), honoring Abraham's willingness to sacrifice his son to Allah. Fortunately Allah intervened and provided a ram instead. Sacrificing an animal is not a skill I plan to use, but a full life leaves room for the unexpected, so I took careful note of how it was done.

The first step is obtaining the animal. Here in Göcek most people raise their own, but those who don't could purchase one at the weekly Sunday *pazar*, where last week small herds of goats and sheep straggled along the river bank, obliviously munching their way through spring grass while waiting to be sold. The number of beasts slain in Göcek—some families killed two—is a sign of the village's prosperity. As the *Turkish Daily News* reported, "Most people can't afford to buy a sacrificial animal any more and will share the purchase price with others, even though only one person can sacrifice a sheep or goat." (Though sheep and goats are most often used, the Koran says that any cloven-hoofed animal can be sacrificed; an ox or even a camel is acceptable.)

People who live in big cities can buy their animals at the local supermarket, and this year could even use a credit card. A large color photograph in *Hurriyet*, a Turkish-language newspaper, shows a line of people waiting at a supermarket checkout counter in Istanbul. In each of the grocery carts stands a live, fat, white sheep. The caption reads, "Supermarket sheep, TL500,000 [about $4] per kilo."

After you get the animal home you must care for it. In Ottoman times this meant not only feeding , but bathing, combing, and decorating them with bows and ribbons, even adorning their horns with gold leaf. If there were any so-adorned animals here, we didn't see them. Traditionally, the hide and at least one third of the meat is given to the poor, one third is given to guests, relatives, or friends, and one third may be used by the household. It is in these gifts that the sacrifice becomes meaningful, for it upholds one of Islam's five pillars, that of giving alms. It also means that you can ride into heaven on the back of an animal that has been sacrificed—apparently this is much easier to do than getting there on your own. Many less-religious and nonreligious Turks shun the bonus of a free ride and do not sacrifice, but instead donate money directly to the poor.

We had long been dreading this holiday, which Turks always refer to by running a forefinger across the throat and adding a descriptive grimace. Not only is there a lot of blood around, but as a guest in the country one is likely to be offered a delicacy one would prefer not to receive. To allay our squeamishness we summoned a protective aura of detached curiosity (Ray took his camera), and walked into the village.

The sacrifice itself is simple: after a ritual prayer the head of the family or someone he designates slays the animal with a long, sharp knife by quickly slitting its throat. This is said to be a humane way of killing. Next, it is necessary to blow up the body like a balloon. This is undignified, but it stretches the skin and makes it easier to remove. These days an air pump is used, but Yusuf says they used to just blow into the animal. After this step the head is cut off and the creature is strung up by its hind legs in any handy tree—not high—and the hide is peeled down and off.

As we wandered through town we saw a half-dozen carcasses in varying states of undress hanging from trees, and I was surprised to see how easily this skinning is done; it looks not much harder than pulling off a pair of too-tight pantyhose. It must be carefully done though, because the hides are valuable. The Constitution Court has ruled that sacrificial hides must be given to the Turkish Aviation Association, but there is continual disagreement about this, as some people think they should be given to whomever one chooses. The important point is that a sacrificial hide cannot be sold or used to pay a debt.

After the hide is stripped off, the viscera are removed and the carcass is butchered. Before we went into town I stood on our back deck and watched Mehmet butcher his family's goat. While it's still suspended from the tree the limbs are separated at the shoulder and hip joints, and then it is split down the back. When it's in manageable pieces it's handed over to the women in the family, who cut it into smaller bits.

And that's all there is to it.

Despite the holiday's grim visage there was an air of happy festivity, and the village was teeming with people, both locals and visitors. Dressed in their best, with the children in new spring clothes (it's much like our Easter in this sense), they sat in cafes or ambled along the promenade, shaking hands and kissing friends and family. Several times during our long circuit (coffee, tea, candy, lunch, greetings, conversation), we were approached by children who solemnly shook our hands and wished us a happy bayram. In return we gave them the customary candy or small change. We spent most of the day in town, sitting in our favorite lookout at the edge of the gray-brick square, and marveling at the socializing and family closeness that is so ingrained in this culture.

Westernization (or modernization if you prefer) infuses an element of schizophrenia here though; at least it feels that way to me. Imagine a well-to-do businessman leaving his big-city office. He wears a Savile Row suit and hand-stitched shoes, and carries a leather briefcase holding a laptop and a cell phone. He steps into his dark gray Mercedes with the tinted windows, pops Yo Yo Ma into the CD player, and pulls onto the multi-laned highway. He drives a mile or so before pulling into a supermarket parking lot where the live sheep he ordered on his cell phone is waiting for him in a grocery cart. An attendant ties its legs and our businessman loads it into the car's trunk and drives home to wife and family. The following morning he begins his long-awaited holiday with the ancient ritual of slitting the animal's throat.

The horns of that sheep—which may or may not have been tied with a bow—are the horns of Turkey's dilemma. Somewhere between eastern mysticism and western pragmatism, between conservative Islamic sharia and liberal secular democracy; between western, economic prosperity, and eastern, economic impoverishment, Turkey struggles to find its identity. I may have learned how to sacrifice a goat on Friday, but I'm a long way from understanding this country.

Curiosity makes ten

April 21

The view from our back deck is of fields and mountains. The fields belong to the farm behind us and are by now quite familiar. The mountains are strangers, sheer peaks of gray stone rising straight up, 800 feet or more, with stark and forbidding suddenness. There are two of these broad peaks, separated by a narrow cleft. Looking at them every day has of course aroused our curiosity, and ever since Ian told us there was a trail, and a village at the top, we've wanted to go and see. A few days ago, we finally did.

The thermometer read 73 and a thick haze partially blocked the sun; perfect hiking weather. We packed a lunch and set off along the dirt road behind the house, to what we call the old village. In Göcek proper most of the old houses have been torn down to make way for modern homes and shops and restaurants. But the low hills bordering the peaks hide a collection of old village houses, some of them tumbledown, but still occupied. This is also the route to the spring where we get our drinking water, so we know it well. Today the scent of orange blossoms drifts on the warm, humid air as we pick our way carefully over the muddy road.

On the left side, half-way along, is a five-foot-high stone wall topped by red geraniums and purple flowering sedum. An old grinding stone dominates a packed-earth yard on the right and further on the remnants of a mosaic floor are visible through a veneer of dust and dirt. The mosaic looks like those we've seen in museums, or as part of protected ruins in Kos and other cities. Could this one too be 2,000 years old? Like them, it is made of tiny flat, black and white stones laid in a geometric pattern that remains distinct, despite age and neglect.

I'm happy to see the wildflowers still blooming; the fields along our route are full of yellow and white daisies—at least they look like daisies—and tiny blue flowers, and thousands of scarlet poppies. We stop at the spring to fill our water bottle and then head toward the cleft in the rock face. But first we pause to say good morning to a man with a load of greenery in his arms, standing at the juncture of path and road.

"*Hoş geldinez!*" he says. Welcome! "Where are you from?"

"America," says Ray. This is probably the thousandth time we've answered this question. Sometimes we say, "Göcek!"

"Ah," he grins. "Amerika *çok guzel.*" This means very fine, or very beautiful, or very good. We point to the flowers and the mountains and reply, "Türkiye *çok guzel* too." He nods and smiles, and we exchange goodbye waves as Ray and I start up the path.

It is only a narrow hint in a thigh-high sea of greenery and wildflowers, but we follow it up a gradual incline, past rocky outcroppings to the break in the cliff. Scrambling over piles of gravel and loose shale we climb at last onto the trail that serpentines up a dry watercourse. Before long the sky is a thin strip of white haze between high rock walls. Shrubs and a few pine trees cling precariously to the sheer face, but the trail is rock on rock. Here and there we see signs of repair and supporting stone walls, and it would be no surprise to learn this trail has been used for a thousand years. There are some caves along the route, their roofs blackened by the smoke of many fires. We climb in near silence, with only the sound of our panting and the crunch of shoes on broken shale to keep us company.

At noon we sit down on comfortable boulders at a bend in the trail and eat our tuna sandwiches. We're near the top now, and can see far out into the bay, over the tops of the closest islands. The sun has broken through the haze but there's a breeze, and it's pleasant sitting here. So far we've seen no one; even the goats, whose droppings are everywhere, seem to have deserted the mountain today. A few sparrows twitter and flap past as we munch. After a short rest

We can see far out into the bay . . .

we continue higher, then traverse a saddle in the mountain where, surprisingly, a sparse orchard of gnarled olive trees grows.

Across a small mossy meadow the trail takes a sharp turn to the left and we head west, still following the dry creek. Now, though, we're near the top of the peaks. The swath of sky is broader, pine trees climb up one side, and we're treading over a soft, thick layer of pine needles. The path becomes fainter, sometimes merging with another. Back and forth across the rocky creek it wanders, still upward. We stop for water, and agree to turn back if we haven't found the village at the end of another hour. But the horizon ahead drops steadily and suddenly we're in a flat, cultivated field of tall winter wheat. The red-tiled roofs and whitewashed houses of the tiny village lie ahead, and following the path straight across the field we find ourselves plunk in the middle of someone's barnyard. After stopping to pet two new black and white puppies, we squeeze between a couple of disgruntled cows and make our way to the road.

"Hey, eeyyay! Aaaaee! You want *su*? You want *çay*?" Water? Tea?

A man and his teenage son hail us from a farmyard on the hill. When we pause, they start pantomiming. They saw me in the field, looking through binoculars at the cliffs beyond, and they pretend to do the same. Then they point to the yard behind them. Neither of us knows what's up, but we follow them to the back of a barn where a horse and a donkey stand munching hay. Apparently they think this is what I was looking at, so we dutifully pet the horse and take turns posing with it for pictures. The men find this immensely pleasing for some reason—maybe it's a special horse—and then, naturally, they invite us for tea. Ray looks to me, and I say, "Oh, sure, why not?"

Before we know it the teenager has collected some chairs and we're sitting in the middle of a hard-packed dirt yard. The Baba, a friendly, white-haired man carrying a two-year old boy, is the first to greet us, followed by his wife, an old woman in layered skirts and rubber flip-flops. She stares unabashedly, while giving us a grin that shows her few remaining teeth. "Welcome," she says. The Baba hollers and a young woman appears, then retreats back into the house to make tea. A few minutes later two more women and a man stroll into the yard, and our party of ten is complete.

None of these people speak English, but it's amazing how well you can communicate with taxi Turkish and a talent for charades. We learn that the family owns a fair amount of land here; the Baba has six children, most of whom live in the surrounding houses; and the little boy belongs to the young woman and they're here from Izmir for the holiday. With the exception of the young mother, who is dressed in conservative city clothing, the women wear the village clothing we've become accustomed to—white headdresses, full print skirts and blouses, pantaloons, and sweaters. Ray recognizes one of them from Göcek's *pazar*, a jolly woman who's so hefty and round her single gold bracelet looks embedded in her arm.

Preparing tea Turkish style takes a long time, but we sit patiently and make what conversation we can. I'm not always comfortable in these situations, but over time I've grown used to sitting placidly with total strangers in less than pristine surroundings. At last a box spread with a newspaper is placed in front of us, and a metal tray filled with many glasses of tea is placed on top. Ray is served first, then the man to my left, then everyone helps themselves. We smile and slowly sip the hot tea in the fragile little glasses and then, custom and manners satisfied, we shake hands with them all and depart, accompanied by multiple *"güle güles."*

We return to Göcek by way of the dirt road, meeting on the five-kilometer walk one car, two motorbikes, a young man, a friendly old woman, and two small boys. Half-way down we see a herd of goats, and looking for the shepherd we spot her sitting high atop a rocky outcrop, weaving on a small loom. It's late afternoon, and we're tired and weary when we finally climb the stairs to the apartment, but a hot shower eases the encroaching soreness of winter-wasted muscles. Later that evening I go out to sit on the back deck and gaze contentedly at the mountains, my curiosity entirely satisfied.

. . . plunk in the middle of someone's barnyard.

The art of doing business

Ray writes: April 28

Tape cassettes, Tang, aerosol hair spray, cans of tuna, travel videos, and classical music CDs. Items found at your major drug chain? Maybe, but these are also some of the free items found shrink-wrapped to Turkish magazines at Zeki's news stand in Göcek.

It was a CD version of Beethoven's "Symphony No. 9" that caught my eye, and for TL 400,000 ($2.95) it was mine, along with two slick Turkish society magazines (one free). Earlier in the week it was a bottle of my favorite *biber sosu* (pepper sauce) and a package of Tang (instructions in Russian, Turkish, French, and English), plus of course, the attached magazine all for a cool TL 100,000. (After ten months of purchasing fresh, local oranges at the *pazar* Karen and I agreed the Tang tasted awful).

Zeki's is a great place to hang out. It's a tiny shop, maybe ten by twelve feet, and family run. Little English is spoken. Zeki also sells newspapers, paperback books (very expensive), post cards, film, maps, travel guides, and swimming fins. During the winter he sells rolls of adhesive-backed foam insulation tape.

We like to peruse the newspapers and magazines, though the selection of English-language publications shrinks dramatically during the winter. With tourists returning to Göcek, though, publications in English, German, and Italian are again available. Yesterday's big story was the election in Britain. The British complained about how interminably long the campaign was—six weeks! Will Americans ever be so lucky?

Another newspaper tells us the United States Congress voted to approve the Ten Commandments (God must be pleased). Then in a puzzling contradiction a judge in the state of Georgia refused an order to remove the same from his courtroom. A confusing story.

This was followed by an article comparing American and Turkish styles of doing business. Calling it "Sunflower Seed Mentality" the TDN reported:

"The Turkish and American approaches to eating sunflower seeds illustrate not only different senses of time, but also different kinds of appetite, and different kinds of enjoyment. A Turkish person gets a bag of sunflower seeds, places a single seed on edge between his teeth and tap, tap, tap, the seed is cracked and split. The meat is extracted, and the shell is spit out. The technique is one of some delicacy, requiring the proper feel for the resilience of the individual shell, and some interesting maneuvers to separate the shell from the meat. The process is slow and usually unconscious, the contents are enjoyed easily, and hunger seems hardly to be a question.

"An American gets a bag of sunflower seeds. He tries to crack a seed but bites too hard and ends up with shell fragments in his mouth. This happens repeatedly, with only an occasional, accidental success. He mutters, 'This is stupid, I'm not a parrot.' The American wants, and is used to, a bag of seed-meats. The shells have been removed and they are salted to taste. All he has to do is put a handful of them in his mouth. Eating is fast, the flavor intense, and satisfying hunger is definitely an objective."

The following ad for a business lunch at the Istanbul Conrad International hotel illustrates how Turkish businessmen are adopting the west's high-speed habits with their own version of a quick business lunch. The ad reads:

"Enjoy the taste of the Business Lunch menu, with the quality of Gülizar Cafe, within 45 minute's service time and relax. We provide free car parking and complimentary car wash, all included in the price, and if lunch is not served within 45 minutes the bill is ours."

Personally, I'm sticking to business lunches in Göcek, where I know I won't be rushed.

Temple of Zeus, Euromos

Finally, Foça

May 5

"Foça is different," says Ziya in January. "You must go there," she adds autocratically. "You will like it."

Then, "When are you going to Foça?" she asks in February; and in March, "Have you been to Foça yet?"

Finally taking Ziya's advice we set out in April for Foça (pronounced Focha), a village on the Aegean coast, about an hour north of Izmir. We rented a car and drove west, pausing at Muğla to pick up three hitchhiking university students—third-year computer programmers on their way to an exam. We were glad we stopped because the students were able to explain the meaning of the many flag-draped cars we had seen parked along the road: they were awaiting people returning that day from the hadj, the pilgrimage to Mecca. The flapping red-and-white Turkish flags decorating the autos made us feel part of a happy highway parade as we passed patiently-waiting friends and relatives and met a stream of decorated cars, midibuses and big-buses carrying the lucky pilgrims home.

After a detour to Bodrum for lunch with Rick and Beverly we returned to Milas and drove west to touch the coast at Didyma and view again the gigantic temple home of an Apollon oracle. We were first here three years ago, and it remains one of Ray's favorite places. He spent an hour taking yet more photos while I sat in the sun by the oracle's well listening for advice or inspiration. None came. I stared at the scrubby, muddy grass, concentrated on the thick marble pillars, and paced up and down the wide, high stairs. Silence. Even the sound of traffic on the nearby road dissipated before reaching the deep inner courtyard, and though a few other tourists ambled through, the temple and the oracle remained quiet. Finally, after a disappointing conversation with a foot-long tortoise who would only say, "keep moving" as he kept munching, we headed for Kuşadasi, our stop for the night.

Kuşadasi is a favorite port for cruise ships and it's the point where passengers disembark for day-trips to Ephesus's famous ruins. It is also the port we entered from Samos, Greece on our first visit to Turkey ten years ago. We remembered it as a busy little town with some charm, but since the main highway bypasses it, we hadn't been here since 1987. The growth since then is astounding. New hotels, apartments, and "holiday villages" now crowd the remembered bare hillsides, and traffic has increased tenfold. We promptly got lost. Eventually, after exploring endless dead ends, we made our way to a *pansiyon* a block from the sea, and went to dinner.

It is a habit of restaurants catering to tourists to employ waiters who also act as shills or touts, standing outside and encouraging the beleaguered and confused traveler: "Come! Would you like tea or coffee? No charge! Look at our menu please. If you don't like our food, you don't have to pay. Sit down sir and lady!"

This occurs even in little Göcek during the season, and we find it humorous or annoying, depending on our mood. It's true that one can usually bring this to a halt by replying in Turkish, "No, thank you" or "We are not tourists," but even that gets old after ten or 15 repetitions. Our evening stroll takes us past a long line of such places but we're saved when a load of wood is abruptly dropped from a wagon onto the sidewalk in front of us. It's a delivery for a *pide* restaurant, to be used for their wood-fired oven, and seeing that it's genuine Turkish, with no touts and no tourists, we step cautiously around the wood pile and sit down and order.

The next day we bypassed the famous ruins at Ephesus and went instead to two nearby sites we hadn't seen before, the ruins of St. John's church in Selçuk, and Meryemana, or Mary's house. Many Christians and Moslems believe that the apostle John came with Mary to Ephesus after the death of Jesus, that she lived here between AD 37 and 48, and that she is buried here. Her "house," therefore, is a focus of pilgrimage, and it sits at the end of a long winding road, high in the hills above the city. It's a peaceful location of gentle terraces under tall pine trees, and I can well imagine her, or anyone, wanting to live here. One terraced plot holds a small, deciduous tree thickly decorated with bits of cloth, paper napkins, and plastic that are tied to its branches; a practice of Moslems hoping for good luck or answered prayers. Some of the bits have fallen off and Ray carefully reties them, hoping for good luck too, perhaps.

Mary's house is long gone but the foundations of the present small, stone chapel are said to date from the first century AD., and two Popes have given the site their blessing. We joined the queue into the chapel, but the steady stream of pushing tourists and devotees with cameras and minicams depressed us, so we left and went to Selçuk.

In our three trips to Turkey we have probably driven past Ayasoluk Hill in Selçuk at least ten times. This time we stopped. Evidence of settlements as early as 2000 BC have been found on the hill, which is now dominated by high castle walls and the columned ruins of the Basilica of St. John. The apostle, who died around 90 AD, is said to be buried here and the church, built by the Emperor Justinian in the sixth century, was one of the largest in existence before its destruction by Tamerlane in 1402. We have to run a gauntlet of souvenir and rug sellers ("I am sorry for the high price of parking; maybe you will come into my shop and sign the book I will send to the government to protest?"), but eventually we enter through the high stone gate.

The view from the site is lovely, the ruins are interesting—though not compelling—and the sunshine and landscaped surroundings make it a pleasant stop that we share with only two other tourists. Much of the marble and many of the columns were expropriated by the builders from Artemis's temple at Ephesus, and standing at the Christian apostle's grave site I wonder if he feels vindicated by this symbolism or merely irritated.

After a quick stop at the Izmir train depot to check on fares and schedules to Ankara (a personal visit being the only way we could get this information), we grab a quick chickie-bob sandwich, and then we're off at last to Foça. The highway out of Izmir is under construction, so after negotiating a sharp 110-degree left turn followed immediately by a 90-degree right—along with three other weaving lines of traffic—we find we have also been negotiated out of our proper lane and onto the wrong road. But it's easier to continue on than to maneuver through that mess again; we'll go by way of Manisa and Menemen.

Our route takes us into farmland, and thirty minutes from the cosmopolitan city we cross a village intersection crowded with horse carts gaily painted with miniature village scenes and driven by farmers wearing plaid cotton turbans. Few women are about but one, sitting in a cart beside the road, quickly covers her face as we pass. Coming into the town of Menemen the car ahead suddenly halts and so do we, to be surrounded by a crowd of young men rowdily line-dancing to the dissonant, whining sounds of a pipe and drum. One waves a tall staff tied with what look like women's scarves, and when Ray rolls down the window to ask what's up, they crowd around the car and laughingly shout, "Army!" Does this mean they're new recruits having a last celebration or new civilians celebrating their release? Either way, they are finding joy in the moment.

After the dancers pass into the realm of the rear view mirror we gather speed, the road straightens and flattens, and at last, in mid afternoon, we enter Foça. And yes, it does seem different.

"Near the beginning of the sixth century [BC]," writes Will Durant in *The Life of Greece,* "the Phocaeans of Ionia landed on the southern shore of France, founded Massalia (Marseilles), and carried Greek products up the Rhone and its branches as far as Arles and Nîmes. They made friends and wives of the natives, introduced the olive and the vine as gifts to France, and so familiarized southern Gaul with Greek civilization that Rome found it easy to spread its kindred culture there in Caesar's time."

Phocaea is now Foça, former home to those who also established Antibes, Nice, and Monaco in France; and Rosas, Ampurias and Maenaca (near Malaga) in Spain. That they were avid sailors is evident, and Foça's ties to the sea remain strong; fishing is still the chief occupation. "Foça," many people assured us, "has the best fish anywhere."

Though the town was founded about 1,000 BC there are few visible ruins. A theater and parts of the city walls were uncovered a few years ago, but most of the ancient town lies under the foundations of the current one, and residents who accidentally turn over a piece of marble are understandably more apt to bury it than report it. We enter Foça on a narrow, cobbled street lined with two- and three-story stone houses, and find parking a few yards from the quay, where blue, white, red, and black fishing boats are tied, and large and small nets are spread for repair and drying.

Fishing boats in Foça

Our hotel, the Karacam, is small and typically Turkish, with minuscule, clean rooms, hard beds, and a friendly staff. It faces the long
street that edges the harbor, and across the street is *küçükdeniz* (small
sea), the smallest of two inlets at the foot of the larger bay. On the opposite shore of *küçükdeniz*, stuck like a short, stubby thumb into the
water, is a little peninsula, the site of ancient Phocaea and now home
to restaurants, shops and houses. On the other side of the thumb/
peninsula lies a larger inlet, *büyükdeniz* (big sea). Further out are scattered small islands, including the Siren Rocks that Odysseus cleverly
managed to avoid. The lure of their seductive voices is apparently no
longer a danger, for tourist boats willingly carry travelers there and
back again.

Feride and Esref, whom we first met in Göcek, are moving from Istanbul to Foça (they've kept a holiday apartment here for several years) and we're anxious to see their "new" 140-year-old stone house. After settling in at the hotel we join them at the Baliçiki, a local hangout that feels more like a San Francisco bistro than a Turkish bar. Then we pile into Feride's white Opal for a quick tour of the town before being taken to see the pièce de résistance, their future home.

Unfortunately they've forgotten the key. We'll have to come back tomorrow to go inside, so we cup our hands against the sun and peer into the interior across 18-inch-wide sills and through old double-glazing. Dusty wood floors, arches over windows, high ceilings, and a narrow wooden staircase are all I can make out, and most of this will eventually be removed. But the two-story building's proportions are splendid, the stone walls solid, and the potential tantalizing. We agree it will make a wonderful home.

Foça contains many old houses like this one, and they are definitely part of its charm. Pale, sturdy stone-block houses with tile roofs, a twist or curve of wrought iron for trim, or a flower box in a window. They are simple buildings with straight, simple lines, and they line the street that skirts the *küçükdeniz*, giving Foça a look of solid respectability and permanence that Turkish villages often lack. The Turkish government has declared Foça a special environmental protection area, and the old stone buildings cannot be externally altered.

One such house, perched on a bluff at the end of the peninsula, contains the apartment our friends are currently living in, and we join them there for a drink, to watch the sunset from their brightly-painted rooms.

"We asked the landlord to let us repaint in more traditional colors," explains Esref, "but he wouldn't permit it. They just use whatever they have handy you know," he adds apologetically.

I like the colors though—they are so outrageous for rooms—
bright blues and yellows and pinks; even the deep, decorative mold-
ings in the high ceilings are dressed in cheerful, gaudy hues that ac-
centuate the view from the window. We sit contentedly with a glass
of wine and watch the sun move slowly toward the watery horizon,
growing steadily larger and more brilliantly red, until the room and
the four of us in it glow with a warm, orange light that lingers for a
moment, before slowly dissolving into evening darkness.

Foça is different. It is certainly not Bodrum, or Göcek, or any
other seaside town we've visited. The fishing boats and the bustling fish market are two obvious differences, for nowhere else have
we seen such a healthy seafood trade. During Ottoman times Foça
remained predominantly Greek. Even after the Turkish Republic was
established in 1923 and the population exchanges were ordered, a
few Greeks managed to stay behind. Their influence remains, and
the town is a pleasant blend of Greek and Turkish cultures.

In conversation with a cafe owner the next day we're told that
Foça's differences are not limited to its appearance.

"The religious people don't like Foça," he says. "They move
here sometimes, but they never stay long. They're not comfortable."

The recent sacrifice bayram produced no sacrifices here, and
despite a well-preserved 15th-century mosque, few attend. I've seen
only a handful of women with covered heads, and the town feels far
removed from Islam and its influences.

Like all coastal towns Foça draws tourists, but so far they
haven't overwhelmed the local culture. Its protected status has kept
the insidious holiday villages from encroaching, though they abound
along the coasts nearby, and many of the tourists are Turks from
Izmir who drive up for weekends and holidays. It is their presence,
probably, that gives Foça its cosmopolitan air.

There is a military base nearby and a large naval presence and on Sunday the streets team with well-behaved sailors and soldiers wandering from tea shop to cafe to otogar, and gazing curiously through shop windows. It is army policy to send young men from western Turkey to the east, and vice versa, so these polite young soldiers are probably from Turkey's eastern, and most conservative provinces. We guess they are poor and we know their salaries are minuscule, and waiting in line at the bank teller machine, Ray watches them saunter away carefully counting out their one or two million lira: $7–$14.

We spend two nights in Foça, and on the morning of the third day we drive east, with only a brief stop at Sardis, which surprised us by being there and by being so utterly different. From Sardis we turn south onto a narrow asphalt/gravel/dirt road and creep past

Ruins at Sardis

remote villages while crossing two 5000-foot mountains just below the snow line. Isolation in Turkey can mean a distance of less than 50 miles. Around 5 p.m. I win my bet and we check into the Aphrodisias Hotel, with the ruins of that city visible from our balcony. (Ray was sure we would have to drive 35 miles back to the nearest town.) There are only two other guests in the sprawling motel-style building, a French couple who are backpacking. In common, unspoken agreement we avoid one another at dinner, but share maps and information over breakfast.

Our first visit to Aphrodisias was ten years ago, on a late December day with the sun about to set. This time I wanted to spend as much time as it took and we did. About four hours, plus lunch, were devoted to the city, and I left with only one desire, to see it again in ten years, when even more has been uncovered.

Aphrodisias is a work in progress, an archeological dig that was directed by a Turkish-American professor from New York University, Kenan T. Erim, from 1961 until his death in 1990. He is now buried at the site. The work has been carefully done, and the reconstructed elements are not marred by the sometimes careless "filling in" that detracts from other ruins. The site itself is an old one, dating to the late Neolithic period, and the Bronze and Iron Ages (ca. 4360-460 BC). It was an important Greek, then Roman, and then Byzantine city, until a 7th century AD earthquake destroyed it beyond repair. It has, it appears, always been the focus of goddess worship.

The ruins are remarkable for many reasons—the blue marble, the almost complete stadium—but what fascinated us most was the sculpture. In contrast to the fate of most Turkish sites, the art found here has not been carted away to grace distant museums. Thanks to Erim's insistence it remains on site in a museum built for the purpose but already growing too small for the rapidly accumulating collection.

Rapidly accumulating because a famous sculpture school existed here for six hundred years—imagine!—and the resulting classical Greek and Hellenistic works are remarkable for both their quantity and quality. Most impressive to us were the faces. The theater and odeon were graced with friezes of theater masks and actors, and a frieze over the mammoth agora gate held more. Now they sit propped on the grass in the museum courtyard: faces of people you know, or would like to know, or would hate to meet in a dark alley: children, old men, lovely women, pans, satyrs, goddesses, warriors. Ray took endless photographs while I wandered from face to face imagining their life stories and considering how little we've changed.

Reluctantly but inevitably we left the glories of Aphrodisias behind and headed over the last mountain pass on the road toward Fethiye and Göcek, arriving home in time for dinner. On the way to the restaurant we spotted a familiar face, and we were happy to be able to call out, at last, "Hey, Ziya! We went to Foça!"

Stowaways

May 13

When Ray woke me with a cup of coffee at 6:15 a.m. I thought for a fleeting moment that it was time to get up and go to work. Old habits. Then I remembered that we were sailing today, going with Bob and Helen to Kaş. Knowing that Bob is nothing if not prompt, I gulped my coffee and put my feet on the cold but righteous path.

We climbed aboard the *Helen Mary V* promptly at 7:30 a.m. and a few minutes later were motoring away from Club Marina under sunny skies, joining a fleet of 42 sailboats on their way east. Bob and Helen are participating in the Eighth Annual Eastern Mediterranean Yacht Rally (EMYR) and were on their way to Egypt. We were stowaways on this day's leg (55 nautical miles), and happy to be aboard. The rally started in Istanbul on April 26, and will finish in Port Said on June 11. Boats have been joining (and probably dropping out) all along the route and 110 are scheduled to sail from Antalya to ports in eastern Turkey, Cyprus, Syria, Lebanon, Israel, and Egypt. But politics, in predictably juvenile fashion, will intervene; those wishing to visit Israel must bypass Lebanese and Syrian ports. The rally is reassuringly international though, with people from twelve nations registered, in boats ranging from 26 to 81 feet.

(*HMV* is 48 feet. Unlike our apartment, where water, electricity, and telephone all have a habit of resting when you most need them to work, everything on *HMV* works; a light even comes on when you open the closet door. I feel shockingly deprived.)

The day is mild but the winds are wildly unsettled and the sea, after we leave the protected Bay of Fethiye, rolls in great, slow, swells. This is the kind of sea that makes people sick, and everyone but me feels queasy. For some lucky reason I'm never seasick; knock on wood. Eventually the waves shrink to low chops, the wind settles into a nice, steady, following breeze, and Bob breaks out the lime- and pink-striped spinnaker. Behind us others are doing the same, and throughout the afternoon we are trailed by a line of six or eight colorful, billowing sails, all the way into Kaş. At one point we catch sight of a lone dolphin swimming off the port side, but despite our pleas she leaves us after only a few showy turns.

The harbor at Kaş is small and the addition of 42 yachts to its normal boat traffic means late-comers have to raft up. This results in strangers necessarily using your boat as a route to shore, and suggests the possibility of interesting encounters. Fortunately *HMV* pulls in early enough to tie up to the dock, next to a small, bedraggled-looking little sloop from Georgia, on the Black Sea. The three men aboard are not bedraggled though, they're having a fine time, and appear un- daunted by the state of their boat or the duty awaiting her.

Kaş's old Greek theater is the site of the EMYR welcome "cock- tail" party, and it's in full swing as we arrive. A local group of tradi- tional dancers and musicians wins earnest applause from the crowd of sailors, then the mayor, a small, mustached man in a shiny gray suit, gives a lengthy welcome speech—roughly and briefly translated by the rally Commodore—whereupon bouquets of sage and rose- mary are presented to each yacht.

After a pleasant meal in Bob and Helen's favorite Kaş restaurant and an evening stroll past beguiling shop windows, we spend the night aboard HMV, tossing and turning to the tune of three competing musical blastfests. About 3:30 a.m., after the last bar blessedly turns off its mega-watt sound system, we sleep. A late breakfast of eggs and bacon—brought from England—and then Ray and I stand on the dock and wave as our friends sail away to view folk dancing and speeches in Finike, Antalya, and points east. Then we turn our attention to a hot and humid Kaş.

We have passed through Kaş several times on our way to and from Antalya, but never stopped. It is, of course (are you tiring of this refrain?), an old town, formerly called Antiphellos, and dating back at least to the 4th century BC. Like most towns on this coast it's squeezed onto a narrow edge of land against 500-meter high cliffs. A few ruins, mostly Lycian tombs, are scattered around town, the most notable sitting at the top of a steep, narrow street lined with shops. This is the principal tourist track, where rug and jewelry and antique stores compete for attention with the buildings they occupy.

These buildings are white-painted Ottoman-period houses, and each has a partially enclosed wooden balcony projecting over the street. They are plain and spare, or decoratively carved, and bougainvillea and other bright blossoms creep over the tops of many. I imagine women sitting with their glasses of tea behind the hiding lattices, cheerfully greeting and gossiping with neighbors across the narrow gaps that separate them. Some of these little porches are obviously new or rebuilt, but they accurately portray the charm of the old style, and provide a pleasant focus for Ray's camera.

Kaş is the point of departure for Kastellorizo, a Greek island that lies only three nautical miles off Turkey's coast. It is one of the smallest inhabited islands of the Dodecanese chain, and the easternmost point in Europe. The island is poor, and for some time it was almost uninhabited. But the growing tourism in this part of the Med is bringing former residents back—most had emigrated to Australia—along with much-needed income. We were hoping to visit Kastellorizo before we started home, but the only boats going would not return until late afternoon, so unhappily we've missed our chance. We've added that miss, however, to our list of reasons to return.

It's hot and we still have a three-and-a-half-hour bus ride ahead, so after a long walk and a light snack we retrieve our luggage from the photo-developing shop where we had parked it and hike up one more hill to the *otogar*. Fortunately and typically we have only a 15-minute wait before the bus departs, so I settle down with my book as Ray goes in search of a cold bottle of water.

The route from Kaş to Patara is spectacular, and though my book is good, it can't compete with the sparkling sea that, from where I sit, appears to lap at the side of the bus. On my right the cliffs stretch steeply upward and the dry, whitish-gray rock and scant vegetation are in stark and dramatic contrast to the cobalt wet on my left. The little bus lurches along the two-lane highway, weaving left, right, up, over, and down the vertiginous-making hills. At one point I feel a sudden, sharp pang of homesickness for this view, though it's there, smack in front of me. Our coming departure is always with us now, and this flash of homesickness, if it can be called that, forces me to think about how comfortable I feel here in Turkey, and how difficult it may be to leave.

About 3 p.m. we reach Fethiye and change buses (another 15 minute wait) and then, before we know it we're back in Göcek, pulling our rolling bag down the now familiar street, and waving hello to now familiar people. The rock-embedded road, the dust and ditches, the half-completed construction projects, the head scarves and clashing prints, the smiles and waves, all reassure me that I'm still in Turkey. Some days are worth getting up for.

The tourists return

May 20

It's a quiet, rainy afternoon here in Göcek. Ray has gone into the village to check on our mail—a dubious exercise since we rarely get any—and I'm curled up with the laptop in one of the big leather armchairs. The Baba brought four big, white calla lilies to the door an hour ago, and I've put them into one of Emma's copper jugs. There's a tempting aroma coming from the oven—peanut butter cookies— and our little apartment feels warm and cozy and homelike. I can't believe it's April, and that our year here is drawing to a close.

Theater ruins at Patara

In the meantime sleepy Göcek continues to delight us with new sights and experiences. Now it is rapidly turning back into the tourist village we found on our arrival. Walking along the waterfront on our way to lunch today, before the rains came, we were surprised to see some of the Sunsail charter fleet—already! The white sailboats, with their bright red, roller-furling sails, were a sudden, startling addition to winter's empty blue sea and the worn, gray *belediye* dock.

Their appearance should not have surprised us. We've watched the workers around town lately, the ones building the new shop-and-office complex, and the others remodeling the *pansiyons* and stores, and they're as frenetic as Turks ever get. And every day another store opens for business. The shop across the street from our lunch stop has added a second room and done its once-a-year dusting, and the merchandise—copper pots, little cast-iron Aladdin lamps, *fezzes* and other caps, and onyx chess sets—looks pretty spiffy.

Our lunch spot, the Halley Doner, will soon be new and improved too. Like every business here the cafe is a family operation, and the three or four outdoor tables facing the square sometimes serve as the family living room. Halley's has had a limited menu over the winter, but it will soon grow from *tost* and meatball sandwiches to *tost*, pizza, *donor kebab* and *pide*. The cafe is a favorite with local expats, and Göcek's British residents and in-port sailors meet here every Sunday afternoon to drink beer and gossip. Our favorite time though, is noon on any weekday, because that's when all the schoolchildren parade by on their way home for lunch.

The parade starts with a trickle of teenagers from the lycee who stroll past looking smart; the boys in white shirts with ties, dark slacks and dark blue blazers, and the girls in narrow blue jumpers and white blouses. Then come the 200 or so grammar school children; always running, racing, pent-up energy in blue dresses or smock-shirts with white embroidered collars. Some of them, recognizing us as foreigners, say a cheerful, "Heh-low!" as they go by. Of course we respond, and then they respond, and typically we go back and forth many times before they, or we, run out of steam.

Today I watched as three little girls on three separate occasions stopped short in their homeward dash, trotted over to the cafe owner's two-year-old boy, who was sitting at the table next to us, and firmly planted a kiss on his cheek before darting off again to join their friends. Each time this happened the little boy smiled broadly and then went back to peacefully munching his bread.

Since many of Göcek's residents are related, the three girls may have been acknowledging a cousin, but this open affection typifies how children are treated and raised here. Though some Westerners say Turkish children are spoiled, I think *coddled* is more appropriate because it denotes a protective affection that seems to me to be the norm. When we first arrived we were surprised to see small children, two, three, and four years old, playing in the square, apparently unsupervised. In fact any adult who happens to be around will care for a child, or discipline him if necessary. And discipline usually means picking up the disruptive child and giving him or her a loving hug and some warning words. I have never seen a child spanked, but I frequently see them hugged, kissed, and caressed by both sexes of all ages. If this is the key to raising the helpful, friendly people we've met here, I think the Turks are on to something.

After lunch we wandered back home down Göcek's single main street. Despite the May 1 construction deadline we're still climbing over piles of sand, scattered lumber, half-filled ditches, and bits of rebar. Even the few tourists who've ventured into town are not

immune to inconvenience. In a perverse way I am happy about
this because I find that I resent their arrival. When I shame-facedly
admitted this to Ray I was comforted to hear that he agreed, even
though he said it was "selfish and silly." As for why we resent them,
I'm not sure. Maybe it's because we have to leave in a few weeks,
and they'll still be here enjoying the sunshine and the friendly people
and the sailing and the restaurants and the wonderful views—and
we won't.

Geez. It's a good thing Ray made these peanut butter cookies.

The Belediye

A long walk to Greece

May 26

The view from this tiny chapel would be familiar to anyone who has traveled in Greece, for like uncounted others it sits remote and alone on a high peak. On one side the mountain drops precipitously away to the Mediterranean, a thousand feet or more below. The flat, featureless sea glistens in the sunlight, and a lone white sail silently emerges from a hidden bay and crosses left to right. Reluctantly turning our backs on this serenity we look down on the old Greek village, a jumbled collection of square, stone buildings spilling across the hillside into one of the lushest, prettiest valleys we've seen in Turkey.

A Greek village in Turkey may seem incongruous, but before 1923 there were many along the Aegean and Mediterranean coasts. This one, the largest of its kind remaining in Asia Minor, is called Kaya Köyü, and it's now deserted. Its residents, with about two million other Anatolian Greeks, were removed to Greece in a forced population exchange, the result of Atatürk's determination to keep Turkey for the Turks.

By all accounts the Christian Greeks and their Muslim neighbors lived peacefully in this valley for generations, and after the Greeks departed the Turks left the village alone. One source says they believed the Greeks had laid a curse on it; others report they felt sympathy for their lost neighbors and left it as a monument. In the 1980s a tour company tried to purchase the property for use as a holiday village, but negative publicity and the Greek-Turkish

Friendship Society succeeded in preventing the sale. The property now belongs to the state. Time and several earthquakes have taken their toll, but two large orthodox churches and two tiny hilltop chapels mark the village irredeemably as Greek.

Just as my sources vary as to why the village has been neither used nor removed, so do they vary regarding the number of former residents. One guidebook states categorically that there are 2,000

Kaya Köyü

houses here, and looking around, we agree with that estimate. Assuming a conservative four to a family, that's 8,000 people. But another book says 3,500 Greeks abandoned the town, and a third states without a blink that Kaya, "was home to tens of thousands." The information sheet handed to us by the jolly woman at the Cavusoglü motel-restaurant-bar-swimming pool says 26,000 people were evacuated from

Kaya. Whatever the number, they left behind what must have been a lovely, prosperous village, and the sight of 2,000 or more deserted, empty houses is saddening.

We got to Kaya Köyü about noon, after hitching a ride from Göcek to Fethiye with three local shop owners who were driving to the city on business. From Fethiye we hiked along a narrow asphalt road that hairpinned uphill, and uphill some more, and again more, before it finally leveled off and dropped into the little valley, called Kaya Cükürü. Despite the warmth of the day and the long uphill it was a pleasant walk, taking us high above Fethiye and its bay, through pine forests and fields of wildflowers. A mile out of town we paused to say hello to an old, toothless man riding a heavily-laden donkey. He brought his beast to a halt, put a hand in the pocket of his sport coat, and carefully handed each of us a single, unshelled almond. Further on we heard a shepherd whistling in the pine trees and saw his goats hopping nimbly from rock to rock; we crossed paths with two sturdy tortoises, three donkeys, hobbled; and a single brown caterpillar making its lonely way across the hot, asphalt road.

Near the top of the hill a nomad's black, goat-hair tent stands hidden in the trees; it's nearly invisible but the bright, flapping laundry gives it away. An old, rock road parallels ours for awhile, and we cut across and walk on its rough, shaded surface until—too soon—it disappears under asphalt. Descending, we're passed by two smartly dressed bicyclists and when we round a bend further on we find them in a wayside taking pictures. A fit-looking German couple who might be in their mid-sixties, they're on a months-long bicycling holiday, staying in *pansiyons* and enjoying daily exploratory rides. After an exchange of bicycling stories and a round of photos they climb on their bikes and zoom off down the hill, their colorful shirts, shoes, and hats marking their progress against green fields, like rolling wildflowers.

There are so many flowers growing in the valley fields of winter wheat or barley that it almost looks as though the flowers are the crop. Scarlet poppies, yellow and white daisies, yellow and red blooming shrubs, blue-blossomed thistles, low, tiny, purple ground cover. Color is everywhere. Blessedly and surprisingly, there is no construction here, only white stuccoed houses, red tiled roofs, neat fields, and bucolic little farmyards; a Turkish *Shangri-la*.

After a disappointing lunch in a too-touristy cafe (we should know better by now), we turn our attention to the derelict village and start the climb to the chapel on the peak. First though, we visit the basilica, a multidomed structure with 1888 spelled out in black-on-white pebbles at the entrance. It must have been lovely, there is a marble screen before the altar, and small, intact frescoes above. Remarkably, some of the faces are still identifiable. We take a quick, obligatory look into the bone depository, where skeletal remains not carried off by tourists are now behind a locked grill. The skulls are long gone, borne away by the Greeks with the rest of their belongings.

Leaving this sadness, I trail Ray up the old rock-paved street.

This village has been deserted for nearly 75 years, and except for the churches we see no roofed buildings. There are stone walls everywhere, jutting at right angles and forming rooms or parts of rooms. A few are intact, but most are partially crumbled. A marble mantle piece has survived over there, and here are daubs of Greek-blue paint spattered across interior walls. But most staircases lead nowhere, and treads support flowers, not feet. The rock streets, so tough and so permanent, have all but disappeared under clumps of blooming shrubbery, rock slides, and erosion.

We spend almost two hours poking among the ruined walls, delighting in the flowers, and imagining the village as it was. Seeing Kaya Köyü it's easy to appreciate how even grand marble edifices like those in Aphrodisias can disappear over time, and despite my love of old marble and historic sites, it's reassuring to see how quickly the earth reclaims itself. Anatolia is a treasure house of such ruins, revealing, layer upon layer, humanity's belief in its ability to create enduring civilizations, each more important and more permanent than the last. More apparent, but for some reason less appreciated, is nature's relentless success at turning that delusion into fields of flowers.

... [he] handed each of us a single, unshelled almond.

You like tea?

Ray writes: June 3

Anyone who has visited Turkey has heard the refrain, "What would you like drink (sometimes "trink"), apple tea, lemon tea, normal tea?" and has seen men and boys delivering small glasses of hot tea on gleaming metal trays. *Çay* is the country's national drink and its consumption far exceeds Turkish coffee. The best tea comes from the Rize area of the Black Sea.

You might be offered tea at any time; as a ploy to get you into a carpet shop or restaurant, in the *pazar*, while shopping for groceries, or while visiting old and new friends. I sometimes measure my day in the village by my tea count. An order for tea is usually placed via an intercom. Most businesses have a little box hanging nearby with a wire leading to a tea kitchen; a button is pressed and the order is given. A more reliable method, one not prone to the electrical outages we experience, is a pull-cord system. A cord is stretched between a business and the tea kitchen on a series of pulleys, and by ringing a bell a prescribed number of times the order is relayed. I've seen these cords stretching several blocks.

Ilhan and his father Ozden run a tea service from a room adjacent to their market, and as I sipped yet another glass of tea he gave me a glimpse of how profitable the business is. His tea service covers about a third of Göcek. On a busy day his young Kurdish employee

Suat delivers up to 500 glasses of tea to thirsty Turks and willing tourists. A glass of tea retails for about 11 cents so on a good day Ilhan takes in about $50. His daily overhead is less than $18, including wages, so in a good month he clears in the neighborhood of $800, minus a few broken glasses. Competition with other tea kitchens is fierce and territories are the norm. With a wink, I call his tea service "Çay Mafia." Blushing, Ilhan winks back.

A gorgon at Didyma

The right to hug

June 9

Göcek is again wearing summer clothes. The tourists are pacing the promenade, the chartered yachts are disappearing and reappearing at weekly intervals, the pink oleanders are in bloom, cherries and watermelons are in the *pazar*, and it seems we've come full circle. It is the way of all places to change and not change, and Göcek, a village much under pressure from tourism, reflects this. There are new façades, new buildings, new businesses, new roads, and a newly extended dock and promenade. The little *feribot* has a new schedule, the Çan restaurant has new tables, and our garden has new fruit trees.

The Göcek *belediye* has not changed. Like a many-headed hydra it sees potential for despoliation in every direction. The winter-built roads are unfinished and unpaved, the new promenade lacks footbridges and trim, the new marina was started and abandoned, and the covered market, under construction when we arrived, still lacks a roof. But a traffic-altering bridge is almost complete, and last week they started hauling dirt from west to east to cover the wetlands (known here as swamps) on the other side of the little river. This anthill of activity appears to have no one in charge, it just charges ahead. A friend here snidely refers to the collective *belediye* as Einstein, and I've concluded that in what passes for Einstein's mind, moving dirt from one part of town to another is the answer to all the world's problems.

Watching our Turkish friends and acquaintances abide this confusion has reminded us how closely intertwined Americans are with government and its actions. We take for granted our access to information and our ability to influence events around us. While neither access nor influence is unavailable to most Turks, there is a sense of inevitability here that is foreign to our nature. When our phone went dead—along with about half the village phones—we immediately started asking questions: Why is it not working? When will it be fixed? Should we report it? To whom? Simple, obvious questions, or so they seemed to us. The Turkish reaction was a shrug of the shoulders and the shared assumption that, "they are probably working on the wires somewhere; it will be fixed soon, don't worry." Fifteen days later we are not worried; it will be fixed soon.

May and June are the months when American tourists come to town (then the British, then the Germans, then the Italians), and we've heard more American voices in the last few weeks than we have in a year of living here. This is fitting, I suppose, since in a few months we'll be surrounded by them. Inevitably, their presence makes us think about home, and the differences between America and Turkey and Americans and Turks.

We find the Turks relaxed, cheerful, hard-working, tolerant, and amazingly honest and helpful. While all descriptions of this sort are to some degree bogus, I will also hazard that Americans are friendly, confident, outgoing, opinionated, and caring. They're also helpful, but by American standards. I can't remember the last time an American closed his shop and walked four blocks with me to make sure I found the bus station, or when a stranger volunteered to call her cousin in New York to make a hotel reservation for me so I wouldn't have to use my phone card, and then volunteered her cousin to help me when I arrived in New York, "no problem"!

Neither would I call us cheerful, relaxed or tolerant.

When I think of Americans I think of porcupines. We rightly value independence and individual rights, but in exercising and maintaining those we've grown prickly. Each hard-won right has become a quill in our natural armor: This quill is my right to vote, this one my right to privacy, this my right to peace and quiet. Over here are my property rights. I have a right to equitable treatment under the law, to go where, when, and with whom I want; to assemble or not, to speak or not. Down here is my right to be served a not-*too*-hot cup of coffee while in my car. There are lots of quills in our armor.

These defensive quills work well, especially if the porcupine has a good lawyer and they don't get in the way of his work—a crucial attribute—but this prickly individualism has caused us to increasingly turn inward, away from our fellows. Who wants to hug a porcupine?

The Turks, on the other hand, love to hug. As Ray has previously written, they are "touchy-feely" people. Children are held and caressed; adults greet one another with kisses and stroll the promenade holding hands, or with an arm about their companion's shoulders. A Turk will willingly share tools, time, and tea with anyone who needs or wants them. They value their democracy and love their country, but they have more faith in their own hard work than in their government's ability to make life better. In America, government is us—at least we want to believe it is. Here, government is a distant Other, sometimes good, more often bad, but seldom omnipresent. Faith, fatalism, and family ties supplant American belief in government and self-reliance. Turks are not loners. They are nosy, gossipy companions, comfortably sharing everything.

The nosy, gossipy villagers who've shared our year here are as curious about our plans as any friend back home, and as our departure draws near we are continually asked, "When are you coming back?" Our response is usually, "Next year," but this is as much a way of assuaging our own sadness as it is a statement of fact. (But as all good propagandists know, if you say something often enough it becomes truth.) In the meantime, we are surprised to find ourselves being treated to lunches, dinners, drinks, and expressions of regret at our departure. This makes leaving harder, but it also provides impetus for our eventual return.

And of course Göcek will continue to hum along with or without us. The restaurant chairs will fill and empty, the white sails will go up and come down, and the *belediye* will continue moving dirt. Maybe when we return the market will finally have its roof. Life is full of such wonderful surprises.

Elvis is alive in Turkey

Ray writes: June 17

Billy Burger Pizza. That's the lunch spot I chose the day I went to Fethiye to transfer money from the Ziraat Bankasi to our travel agent's account in Istanbul. I was paying for our air tickets from Istanbul to London. The reservation had been made by email, but as with most Turkish businesses, credit cards are not welcome.

Billy runs his little sidewalk restaurant with the help of his pregnant wife and Ardal, a young man in his twenties. I don't remember if it was the delicious looking chicken *donor kebab* or the Elvis music that first attracted me, but over lunch I learned that Ardal has a collection of 500 Elvis tapes, 40 CDs, and more than 1000 photos of the King. Ardal plays Elvis music 24 hours a day and I must say many of the tapes sound like it.

Ardal had trouble controlling himself when I told him I saw the King perform 20 years ago in Eugene, Oregon. He offered me a special banana liqueur and showed me his prized possession—an Elvis/Tennessee license plate.

Chicken *kebab*, Fanta, mixed salad, and all the Elvis anyone could ever want—TL400.000 ($2.79) at Billy's. Such a deal.

Up river through green water

June 20

Dalyan has always been on our list of places to see, but its proximity to Göcek made it a low priority, something we could do anytime. Like New Yorkers who never visit the Statue of Liberty, we seemed destined never to visit Dalyan. But with the advent of our penultimate week here, we realized it was time to make the trip.

The dolmuş dropped us a block from the water and the boats that make Dalyan so popular with tourists. We had planned to hop aboard one of the many tour boats that ply the river, but at the last minute we changed our minds and hired a boat "just for us." It was an affordable luxury and worth it, for we could dictate the day's agenda. Our captain was an agile young man in his 20s and his boat was a 30-foot, old, wooden fishing dinghy, well spruced for the tourist trade, with multiple layers of blue and white paint blunting its once-sharp edges, and a striped kilim over a plywood floor covering its sturdy ribs. Nautical-blue bolsters padded the bench seats on either side, and a matching awning protected passengers from the sun. We climbed aboard, our leader cranked the noisy, two-cylinder diesel engine, and we were off.

The Dalyan river runs north and south, linking the big Köycegiz Lake to the sea. Centuries ago this lake was another Mediterranean bay, but silt and the shrinking, retreating sea choked the entrance, leaving access only by way of the short Dalyan river and acres of reed-filled swamp. Our boat chugs up river through green water. On one side high, gray cliffs line the bank, on the other a flat expanse of farmland stretches away to hills a few miles distant. The morning air is cool and pleasant, and for the moment we have the river to ourselves. We pull the blue cushions onto the white-painted prow and stretch out in the sunshine.

Our first stop is at the mud baths, guaranteed to cure rheumatism, increase male potency, and make one look younger. Photographs of happy bathers covered with dry, gray mud are posted outside tourist bureaus from Marmaris to Antalya. We were not keen on joining them, but we wanted to see it nonetheless. There are two small pools at the site, one with lots of mud and the other full of hot, sulfur-smelling water. Flagstone surrounds the pools, and steps lead up to a covered area crowded with tables and chairs. A boatload of tourists has arrived ahead of us, so we sit and watch as 30 or 40 people of all shapes, sizes, and ages step down into the muddy pool.

This must be some childhood fantasy, plastering your entire body with mud—few seem immune to its charms. Technique, however, var-

Ray plays in the mud.

ies. Some mud lovers are deliberate; calmly and carefully covering every inch of themselves. Others are giddy tossers, scattering and spreading handfuls of the stuff wherever it lands. Partnerships are popular and serious spreaders and tittering tossers pair up to mutual advantage. Covered at last they emerge giggling to face the sun and dry, like gray, withered sunflowers.

I am not convinced by this spectacle and head for the hot sulfur water instead. Ray tries the mud half-heartedly, but apparently he too prefers sulfur, for he soon joins me. We stretch out in the evil-smelling water, close our eyes, and relax. Soon another big group arrives, so we give up and head for the changing rooms—oversize woven baskets—and back to our waiting boat.

From the baths we turn south toward the sea, following the high cliffs past the riverside restaurants of the town, and around a deep bend toward the ruins of Kaunos. On the right, carved high into the steep rock face, are three groups of ancient Lycian-style tombs. They range from rough, unfinished holes in the rock, to elaborate, pillared doors under pitched roofs. The largest, with four pillars, is unfinished. The roof, the capitals, and the tops of the pillars are complete, but they merge into sheer rock only a few feet below. Why is it not completed? Did its wealthy owner move away? Run out of money? Never die? These questions plague me but there is no relief; our captain doesn't know.

From the tombs the river turns away from the cliff face and enters the broad, swampy delta leading to the sea. Tall grass and reeds, some as high as 20 feet, line our passage, and channels spread and twist in all directions. Through the reeds we glimpse the red of a Turkish flag flying atop the mast of the boat ahead of us, but our world is saturated in shades of green. At one point the channel widens and we pass over a large net suspended between two wooden shelters on stilts. After we pass through men on either side turn wooden wheels, raising the net behind us. This is the "fish corporation," says our guide, and before long we see wire ponds full of nursery fish, bass and gray mullet and red crabs, and then the long wooden dock that leads to Kaunos.

My guidebook says that excavations of ancient Kaunos began in 1967, with labor supplied by the nearby open prison in Dalaman (where the prisoners also run an excellent chicken restaurant). We see no workers today, but signs of their labor, in the form of trenches, are visible. Kaunos was founded in the 9th century, B.C. by the Carians (who also founded Halicarnassus/Bodrum). The major visible ruins are a theater, Roman baths, a Byzantine chapel, and an ancient temple. A thick-walled fortress sits high atop an overhanging hill, and remnants of the city walls can be seen in the distance. Most of Kaunos is still buried, but in one deep trench we see an intact stone wall, its huge blocks still perfectly aligned. It must have been a lovely city, surrounded on three sides by water, but now it's uninspiring; or maybe we've finally had our fill of ruins. After an hour of exploring we're happy to climb aboard our private launch and chug chug away through the winding channels, confident that our captain, at least, knows where he's going.

This feels like a ride at Disneyland, except that it is real and the boat engine is noisy. Occasionally a big fish clears the water, or a bird soars overhead, but the green water and the tall green reeds are our primary entertainment. In 20 minutes or so we reach Turtle beach, a spit of sand separating the delta from the sea. The dock is filled with boats like ours, and larger, for this is the point where passengers off the big day-boats from Fethiye and Marmaris board smaller river boats for the trip upstream. It's early afternoon and each arriving boat releases another buzzing flock of tourists.

This beach is famous as the nesting ground of loggerhead turtles *(Carretta carretta)* and ten years ago it was threatened by development. Thanks to the efforts of Greenpeace and conservationists around the world, the beach is now protected during the nesting months of May through October. At least it's supposed to be. Signs warn people to avoid sunbathing in the nesting area and heavy wooden posts clearly delineate it. Boats are no longer permitted to bring tourists here at night when the turtles lay their eggs. But there were people sunbathing in the restricted area and determined tourists undoubtedly make their way here after dark. Our young captain, who was born and raised in Dalyan, says he supports Greenpeace and thinks the protection is a good idea. But with tourism increasing so dramatically saving the beach and the turtles may be a lost cause.

We don't dally at the beach; it's crowded and noisy and depressing, and we're hungry. Besides, the weather is changing: there are high thunderheads moving down from the north. Retreating back to the dinghy, we start our winding trip back to Dalyan. There are more boats now, big, broad ones with rows of benches filled with hot, sunburned travelers. We smugly luxuriate in our spacious craft. Despite the threatening clouds the sun is warm and the green water and crowding reeds and beat, beat, beat of the diesel lull us into somnolence.

Ninety minutes later, alighting from our midibus in Göcek, we find wet streets and puddles of water spreading everywhere. It appears we missed a mighty downpour, an event unusual for this time of year. We have enjoyed typical traveler's luck regarding weather this year, as in, "This weather is really unusual, you should have been here last year." We're not complaining though, we've now managed to do almost everything on our list. All that's left is the packing.

Farewell Türkiye

The question that had dogged us since our arrival, what to do when our year here was over, dogged us still. We delighted in the unhurried life and dreaded returning to the high-stress, competitive world we'd left behind. The proceeds from our house sale were invested in a giddily rising stock market, and despite withdrawing cash for living expenses our nest egg had grown. We felt rather smug about this though of course it was sheer luck. If we continued to spend carefully and live simply, could we *not* work for another few years? Could we in fact hold out until Ray's retirement kicked in? It was a tempting option.

We thought too about spending a second year in Göcek, but that idea was soon rejected. We loved the people and the off-season persona of the village, but the crush of summer tourists and the growing commercialization were less appealing. Shortly before our departure we had dinner with Ziya and her ex-husband, and watched the construction of a big new hotel from her living-room balcony. Her view had once been of quiet lanes and vegetation; now it was cement and breeze-bricks and 24-hour lighting and noisy equipment. Rumors that 800 new hotel beds would soon be available meant little Göcek could not long remain the same.

We left the village with mixed feelings. We were looking forward to our next adventure, to camping in France and housesitting in England. And we looked forward to seeing family and friends again. But it was sad saying goodbye to people we had come to care for and might not see again. Their lives were busy and growing busier though, and we knew that despite all their kind words our year-long stay would soon be just a single whitecap in the growing tide of tourists and strangers making their way to our village by the sea.

June 24

I write from the roof-top terrace of an Istanbul *pansiyon*. On my right is the Bosphorus and its opposite shore, the coast of Asia and Anatolia. In front of me is a section of old Byzantine city wall, with one ivy-covered tower standing higher than its surroundings, its height made more conspicuous by the tree growing from its top. On my left, 1,500-year-old Aya Sofia dominates, her faded red walls and massive gray dome awe-inspiring despite years of neglect. Between the ivy-covered tower and Aya Sofia is an old, old haman, or Turkish bath. There is no plaque, no acknowledgment of its long history, no effort at reconstruction. It's just there, decaying, in the middle of a neighborhood of rundown houses and restored hotels; a neighborhood in endless transition.

Our own transition, from Göcek to Istanbul, was made a few days ago in two stages. The first was by big-bus—a pale blue one with navy and green geometric designs painted on its sides. The bus seats were covered with purple plush accented with red and green checks, and the plush ceiling was a nice rose color. The curtains and headrest covers were tinted a pale shade of lemon. It's hard to feel sad or depressed surrounded by color like this and we didn't. All big-buses in Turkey, at least so far as I can determine, are painted uniquely. Unlike American and European transport companies that choose corporate colors and stick to them, buses in Turkey are painted, seemingly, for fun. Abstract designs and pastel colors cover most of the current crop. Midibuses also enjoy variety, but usually on a basic white ground; dolmuses express their personality with elaborate good-luck charms. The big-buses, however, like Turkey's carpets, the village women's clothing, and the old wall tiles, are a riot of color and pattern.

We spent one night in Izmir, where our favorite hotel continues to be slightly run down, then took an overnight ferry to Istanbul. This was a big-boat; we had a cabin to ourselves, with our own WC. It was pleasant, and a relaxing way to arrive in the busy metropolis. The city is as we remembered it, full of contrasts and contradictions, and people and traffic. Ten million people now live here, from Turkey's richest to Turkey's poorest. Hawkers selling slices of watermelon compete with new BMWs for a piece of the street and a piece of the action. Good Muslim women, covered head to toe in black yaşmaks rub shoulders with modern teenagers cantilevering down the sidewalk on high platform shoes; tourists in sandals, searching for bargains, ignore them all. Yesterday we revisited the glories of

Istanbul waterfront

Topkapi, today we trudged uphill to the spice market. There is never enough time in Istanbul, which means there's always a reason to return.

Tomorrow we board an airplane bound for England and regretfully say goodbye to Turkey. After one short year I cannot say I understand the country, but even the Turks shake their heads and shrug their shoulders occasionally. A year ago, just before we arrived, a new parliamentary government was formed, led by Necmettin Erbakan and Tansu Çiller. But Erbakan's religious party proved too much for the secular military and business leaders, and last week he reluctantly resigned. Much to Çiller's chagrin, Mesut Yilmaz (ANAP) has been asked to form a new government. The army did not step in, as many feared and a few hoped, and democracy has been given yet another chance. This is a critical time for the country, however, and we leave it with some fear for its future.

Göcek's future as a yachting haven seems assured, but it too is changing. Two new hotels will be added in the coming year, and the village will continue to grow. We're glad we learned to know it when we did.

No individual year of living anywhere is without its problems, but this year ours have been minimal. No strife, no illness, no suffering, no struggle. Only occasional frustration from trying to live a 20th-century life in a 19th-century country. But that frustration taught us that conveniences really are conveniences and that, if necessary, we can do without. Turkey has also taught me patience (though I still have far to go), and an appreciation for what it means to live in the present moment. This, and the warmth and hospitality of the Turkish people, are the best possible gifts. They will remain forever in our hearts, and they take up no space in our overcrowded suitcases.

Footnotes

1. Turkey had long struggled with inflation. When we arrived in July, 1996, one U.S. dollar bought 81,792 Turkish Lira (TL). In January it was up to TL106,632 and when we left in June, 1997 a dollar bought TL144,373. During this period banks were paying more than 70% interest on savings accounts in TL. On January 1, 2005 Turkey issued a new currency, dropping six zeros and leaving the TL worth 75¢ U.S. In early 2009 one TL cost 60¢ U.S.

2. In the spring of 1997 the military, which views itself as the protector of Ataturk's secular vision, was pressuring the coalition government to institute reforms that would reduce the influence of the religious right. Among these reforms was a plan to institute compulsory eight-year education. When Erbakan resigned in June, 1997 the eight-year plan was passed by the legislature. This will greatly reduce the number of children attending religious schools.

3. A few days after returning home from this trip we learned there had been some confusion over when daylight-saving time would end, and we had erroneously set our clocks back two weeks too soon. The only clue we had was the mix up over the hour of Bodrum's departing ferry. So little does time matter to us now.

Glossary

Allahaismarladik—goodbye (also, güle güle)

bayram—holiday

belediye—a municipal government

borek—a thin layer of pastry, usually wrapped around various fillings and served hot.

ekmek—bread

evet—yes

gület—a traditional wooden sailing boat, now used primarily for taking tourists on coastal trips in the Aegean and Mediterranean.

hayir—no

merhaba—hello

müezzin—an Arabic word, a corruption of *mu'adhdhin*, meaning he who recites the *adhan* (call) to prayer, a five-times-a-day event.

nasılsınez—how are you?

pansiyon—a pension or small guest house

pazar—a bazaar, or market, usually a weekly affair held out of doors and selling everything from fruits and vegetables to clothing and tools.

pekmez—a sweet, molasses-like liquid made from grapes.

pide—a type of pizza, usually filled with a mixture of minced meat and spices, folded over along two sides for form an oblong shape, baked in a wood-fired oven.

Ramazan—a month-long period of the Moslem calendar devoted to fasting and contemplation. Known in the Arabic world as Ramadan.

teşekür ederim—thank you

Pronunciation guide

Turkish is relatively easy to pronounce once you know that every letter is pronounced and each letter has only one sound. Most letters are spoken as they are in English, but the combinations "th" "sh" and "ch" are not pronounced in Turkish. You can find more information about the Turkish language at many Internet sites.

Letters using diacritical marks, with their pronunciations:

İ, i — (dotted] as "ee" in seen

I, ı — [undotted i] "uh" in plus

Ö, ö — same as in German (ur)

Ü, ü — same as in German, or French as in tu

C, c — pronounced like English "j" as in jet

Ç, ç —"ch" as in churn

G, g — hard as in got

Ğ, ğ — silent (this is the only exception to the
       "pronounce every letter" rule)

Ş ş — "sh" as in shadow

Place names used in the text

Göcek—sounds like go-jek

Muğla—moola

Ortaca—ortaja

Foça—focha

Kuşadası—kushadasi

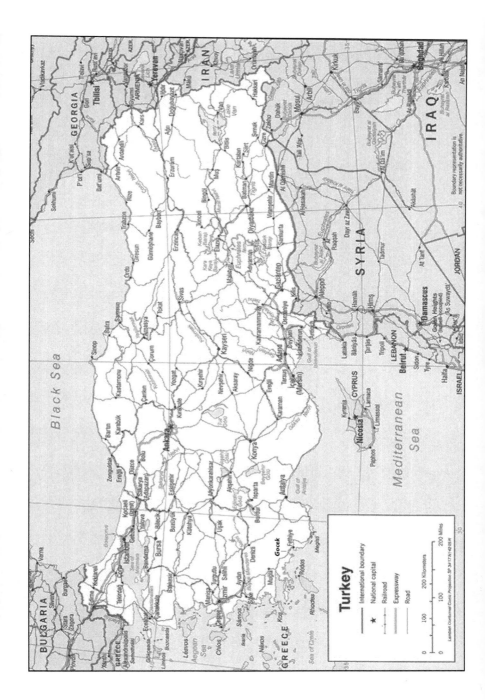

217

7515536R0

Made in the USA
Lexington, KY
30 November 2010